The Chit'lin Controversy:

Race and Public Policy in America

Lorenzo Morris
Charles Henry

University Press
of America™

Copyright © 1978 by

University Press of America™
division of
R.F. Publishing, Inc.
4710 Auth Place, S.E., Washington, D.C. 20023

Library of Congress Catalog Number: 78-50688
ISBN: 0-8191-0471-X

TABLE OF CONTENTS

CHAPTER I

The Choice: The Politics of Race and
Education as a Short-Order Menu

INTRODUCTION

A Negro of Washington, D.C. could scarcely
believe his eyes when he read in the newspapers that Jim Crow had been ended in the
restaurants of his city. He was overjoyed.
He had never expected to live to see the
day. Since the miracle had happened, however, he decided to experience it for himself—at least once. But he would not act
too hastily. The change-over was bound to
take a little time. He decided to wait
three weeks.

Then one Sunday evening he put on his
best clothes, caught a taxi and directed
the driver to one of the most elegant restaurants he knew.

He was greeted with a smile at the door
and again inside, where the waiter gave
him his choice of locations and placed a
handsome menu in his hand. The Negro put
on his glasses and began reading attentively.
He perused the menu so long, in fact, that
the waiter, still courtesy itself, came
over and asked if he was ready to order.

The Negro looked perplexed. "I don't
see any chitterlings here," he said.

> "No, I'm afraid we don't have any
> chitterlings," the waiter agreed.
>
> Once more the customer scanned the
> menu. "How about turnip greens and ham hock?"
>
> Puzzlement turned to frustration on
> the face of the desegregated Negro. "I'd
> like to order black-eyed peas and hog jowl."
>
> "We don't have that either," the waiter
> told him sadly.
>
> The Negro put his glasses back in
> their case, pushed his chair back and rose
> slowly. 'You folks,' he observed thought-
> fully, 'you folks just ain't ready for
> integration.'[1]

It has been at least a decade since stories of restaurant
integration at the end of the black man's dietary rainbow constituted a novelty in popular conversation. If it did not happen
in 1619, when the first slaves were brought to this country; if
it did not happen with DuBois and Booker T. Washington, then by
1954 the nation had certainly begun to accept black people as full
participants in its social and political life. After all this
time, however, complete integration has not been achieved. But
this should surprise no one. As the black man said, "you folks
just ain't ready." Perhaps he is not ready either.

Let us suppose that this man left the restaurant and turned
to black nationalism, as many demonstrators did when they dropped
their picket signs, bandaged their dog bites, and soothed their
battered egos. Now he assumes that integration will never be
more than an empty slogan, and still he is likely to face a similar disappointment. That is, first, nationalistic goals may seem
far from realizable, and second, the nationalistic movement may
well not be just what he had in mind.

The black struggle has included many contradictory movements,
both apparent and real. White and government policy have kept
pace with equivalent contradictions of their own, whether segregationist or liberal. Change can certainly evolve out of these
contradictions, but we must understand them in order to recognize
and promote change. Moreover, the problem for us is not so much
that racial change has not occurred (and it has not), but rather
that as a nation we would not know it if we saw it.

Is it integration when a middle-class black can eat in a
white-owned restaurant, or when most blacks of every social class

2

eat there? Is it nationalism when blacks have restaurants of the
same "caliber" as whites, or must they be distinctive and for
blacks only? If chitterlings are on the menu is the restaurant
likely to express integrationism or nationalism? We do not propose to resolve the "chit'lin controversy," but we do expect that
the formula developed here for dealing with racial questions in
political policy will be applicable in these less critical areas.

The relationship between problems of race relations in public/
private facilities like restaurants and relations in public education is more than metaphorical. The unresolved questions raised
by the simple limitation of choices in the restaurant menu are
parallel to those raised by program and curricular limitations
in the school system. In the latter case, however, the separa-
tist-integrationist controversy has been preoccupied almost ex-
clusively with the forms or format in which blacks might enter
into the educational choice structure. The real educational
policy questions of how the choices may have been previously
structured and how blacks might want to restructure them have
scarcely been posed. The fundamental issues of desegregation
seem to have slipped from view in the transformation of black
protest demands into civil rights legislation. The question of
whether one "gets through the door" of the restaurant or the
school has unfortunately obscured the primary question of what
one is allowed to do after admission. The answer to this question,
as the above ancedote suggests, may dramatically change one's
position on the legislative question. What we therefore propose
to do is to return to the more substantive issue behind civil
rights, "the menu" or the structure of public education.

In the United States, as in all societies, schools have
performed two crucial functions. They have socialized new generations into the prevailing culture, and they have trained the young
for the market place. The United States has not gone as far as
nations like the Soviet Union and France in imposing a national
curriculum, and the subtlety of American political and ecomonic
influence on the public education system has often led to unrealistic expectations about what might be accomplished through the
present structure.

At the outset educational systems were decentralized with
each colony, and usually each community, controling its own schools.
In the South education was the prerogative of a small white elite,
while in the North private schools catered to the wealthier classes
and public education was associated with being poor. By the mid-
1800's, industrialization and a large influx of Irish immigrants
led educators like Horace Mann to propose state support for public
schools. With state support came centralized control that would
help maintain morality and decent behavior, as well as contribute to economic growth. Decentralized control was no longer

3

suitable because it often left the conduct and curriculum of schools in the hands of the very working class that had to be transformed into moral and decent members of an industrializing economy.[2]

For blacks the situation was significantly different. Their position at the bottom of the economy was fixed and the educational system proposed little in the way of economic change; however, the hope of uplifting Negro morals and behavior remained. For the first fifty years following the Civil War it seems clear that there were two educational policies--one white and the other black. The Freedman's Bureau opened over 4,000 very modest schools in the South immediately following the War. The Bureau abandoned most of its educational efforts by 1870. The grand total of $5 million--$1.25 per capita--had been spent to compensate for 200 years of enforced ignorance. In higher education this dual educational policy was just as readily apparent. The Morrill Act of 1862 made no special provision for Negro colleges and only three southern states had designated Negro schools as recipients of federal funds under the land-grant program. In 1890, the Congress enacted a second Morrill Act that forbade discrimination and required that land-grant monies be distributed among blacks as well as whites. The practical result of this fiscal equality was the transformation of academically oriented black colleges into institutes that stressed the vocational training thought to be suited to Negro capacities by state governments using land-grant monies. This program of vocational education was rounded-out with the passage of the Smith-Lever and Smith-Hughes acts of 1914 and 1917 which created a county-agent bureaucracy to oversee the proper vocational instruction of blacks.[3]

The principle of separate but "unequal" was in vogue long before Plessy v Ferguson, as Populist demands led to state laws which shifted the apportionment of funds for schooling from the state to local town officials who used their own discretion in deciding what was "just and equitable." Other states followed the lead of the United States Congress in the District of Columbia in allotting tax money to black schools only in proportion to receipts from black taxpayers. "Certification" laws were developed which enabled the states to pay less to black teachers than to whites, while class sizes were made larger to accommodate the increasing numbers of black children seeking schooling. Whites in the Black Belt gained the most from these arrangements because the increasing black enrollment qualified each county for more funds based on total enrollment, but the money never reached the increasingly burdened black schools.[4]

In the light of the history of black education in this country, it is not surprising that the school system has failed to alter significantly the economic or social status of the majority of

4

blacks. It is undoubtedly true that education has generally been regarded as the primary rung of advancement on the American ladder of social mobility. Demographer Philip Hauser asserts: "Without question, the major factor in the assimilation of the white immigrant groups who came to this country--the 'Americanization'-- was the school."[5] More to the point, Herbert Gintis argues that schools developed certain behavioral attitudes that made the immigrants "desirable" workers. According to Gintis "schools affect earnings by creating an internal 'social structure' whose authority, motivational, and interpersonal relations are designed to replicate those of the factory and office."[6] Milton Gordon sees education as the crucial institutional area linking the ethnically mixed political and economic realms with the ethnically closed areas of religion, family, and social functions.[7] The failure of the schools to act as the "great assimilator" and "job trainer" for blacks to the same extent that they did for ethnic groups either forces one to accept notions of black genetic inferiority or to challenge the supposed racial neutrality of American educational policy.

In the discussion of racial policy as opposed to the analysis of race itself, the concept of culture has received considerable attention in immigrant-group studies. White Americans have, without reliance on careful studies, traditionally viewed integration in cultural terms. The myth of the "melting pot" society has been widely believed with little concern for examining its validity. Immigrant groups arriving in "the land of freedom" are expected to surrender their cultural freedom, and assume the mannerisms of the dominant group, unless of course they choose to remain "a tired, wretched, and poor group." The more readily Anglo-Saxon culture has been adopted, the more quickly the group has been assimilated. Of course, complete assimilation has seldom, if ever, occurred, and many ethnic groups have retained substantial traditional cultural attributes. Moreover, some immigrant attributes have received the "good house-keeping seal of approval" by being incorporated in the dominant culture.

Blacks, however, presented a special problem to the assimilation-minded American, first because the original purpose of their importation was quite the opposite of assimilation--that is, blacks, were expected to be "tired, wretched and poor," as a result of exploitation. Secondly, blacks were perceptibly different in appearance. Historically, this physical difference led to biological and genetic arguments to justify separate and discriminatory treatment. The exploitable position of blacks in America by association, turned a physical difference into a measure of physical virtue. Thus, many whites deluded themselves into believing that the Afro-American lacked the physical and mental capacity to adopt the dominant American culture or any real culture. Moreover, it was feared that any assimilation of blacks would

5

unleash a rash of counter-evolutionary intermarriage. It has only recently been recognized by white Americans that blacks were not waiting with panting eagerness to marry their sons and daughters.[8] Along with this limited recognition, the federal government has initiated programs to aid the "culturally disadvantaged" regardless of physical appearance. Yet, despite this new liberalism, the disadvantaged are still identified on the basis of physical appearance and not on a cultural basis.

The government and social action groups and even individuals have taken positions on racial issues which we can call their racial political policy. In large measure, racial political policy, like dietary policy, is a matter of individual values; and we would not argue that anyone should change his mind about either, however bigoted or overweight he might be. This, the normative aspect of one's values on race, has been eloquently, though unproductively, debated for centuries. Yet, there is another, cognitive aspect of human values which has been too often ignored. There is presumably no cognitive problem in our attitude toward food, as long as we concentrate on its nutritional quality. When, however, we confuse food with, for example, motherly love, as psychologists warn, then our dietary policy becomes unrealistic. As for race, there is significant disparity in our cognitions; we don't know or agree on what it means to be black or white. A single policy will be unrealistic and several policies will not come together unless there is agreement on the identity of the subject in question--race.

Pierre van den Berghe notes that the term "race" has been quite confusing because of its four principal connotations.

> 1. Physical anthropologists have called races the various subspecies of <u>homo sapiens</u> characterized by certain phenotypical and genotypical traits (e.g., the "Mongoloid race" or the "Negroid race")...
> 2. Laymen have profusely used the word race to describe a human group that shared certain cultural characteristics such as language or religion (e.g., the "French race" or the "Jewish race").
> 3. Race has been loosely used as a synonym for species (e.g., the "human race").
> 4. Many social scientists have meant by race a human group that defines itself and/or is defined by other groups as different from other immutable physical characteristics...[9]

Physical anthropologists cannot agree among themselves on the
number of biological classifications under the first meaning and
the third meaning is too broad to have any relevance here.
Van den Berghe uses the fourth meaning to refer to a group that
is socially defined but on the basis of physical criteria. This
may be distinguished from the second meaning which is commonly
used to designate "ethnic groups" and socially defines race on
the basis of cultural criteria.[10]

Van den Berghe's recognition of the social base of racial
cognition is useful and sets him apart from social scientists
who choose to ignore or confuse the distinctions between racial
and ethnic groups. For example, George Simpson and J. Milton
Yinger, in their widely used text Racial and Cultural Minorities,
attribute behavioral differences between blacks and whites in
the United States to " (1) class, educational, occupational, and
other nonracial factors and (2) the somewhat different 'social
world' in which the Negro lives because of racial segregation
and discrimination."[11] Their refusal to recognize the socially
defined nature of both individual and group self-consciousness
and the built-in structural biases that it creates leads them to
reject any distinctions between cultural and racial policy. Their
approach is reflected in a critique of Oliver Cox's much neglected
work--Caste, Class and Race. In that work Cox makes the following
distinction:

> Anti-Semitism is an attitude directed against
> the jews because they are jews, while race
> prejudice is an attitude directed against
> Negroes because they want to be something
> other than Negroes. Probably the clearest
> distinction between intolerance and race pre-
> judice is that the intolerant group welcomes
> conversion and assimilation, while the race-
> prejudiced group is antagonized by attempts
> to assimilate.... [12]

Jews were anti-social because of their unwillingness to part
with their cultural heritage. Negroes were regarded as sub-social
as a result of their genetic inferiority. Simpson and Yinger
reject Cox's distinctions between religious persecution and racial
domination because they "block our ability to see interconnections."[13]
It is our contention that only through the recognition of these
distinctions, both normative and cognitive, that relationships
between racial groups and racial public policy can be understood
and hopefully predicted.

Ask any American to what race he belongs and he is almost
certain to know. More importantly, he probably feels it or

7

senses it so deeply that he has never thought to question it. Because we sense our racial identity much as we sense our existence, we tend not to ask how we know that we are black or white, as we do not ask how we know that we exist. Governments and organizations do not make policy that deals broadly with existence, but they do make racial policies.

You can not see that I am black and you are white, or vice versa, but merely see that I reflect less light than you or we have different facial features. Even where one defines race in purely "physical" terms, some variable interpretation of the sensory data is implicit. There must be a "reason" for making physical appearances the point of departure for social policy which goes far beyond the physical. The most evident reason or rationale behind an individual's racial awareness may well include a normative aspect of unreasonable prejudice. Beyond or beneath this prejudice there is a cognitive value position concerning race through which one's beliefs become reality; that is, through which he or she seeks to implement his or her beliefs. Social critics have dealt more with simple prejudice than with its cognitive basis, and have not changed nearly enough minds. Perhaps, everyone's cognition of race includes a physical element, but it is frequently not limited to the physical.[*] It includes often too what may loosely be termed states-of-mind concepts of race. An analogy: we have tended to describe others as drunk when their observable behavior indicates a deviant state of mind; and it is only possible for one to see himself as drunk when he judges his own actions by standards, memorized or ingrained, other than those toward which his present state of mind inclines him. Similarly, physical criteria are judged as indicative of something other than what we mean by black and white according to some external standards; standards expressed in social behavior and understood as states of mind.

Depending largely on the persistence and proliferation among a group of people, these states of mind become cultural characteristics. Accordingly, the perception of someone with a different skin color is insignificant except for the behavior one thinks usually accompanies the skin color. Importantly, however, the observer recognizes that the racially characteristic behavior is only statistically coincident to the skin color. Thus, race becomes significant (meaningfully existent) through the conceptual

---

[*] Where we are referring to the racial cognate as purely physical, cognition is still mediated by the selective subconscious organization and ordination of sensory data involving social phenomena only in a remote and developmental sense.

mediation of two states of mind; i.e., the observer's consciousness
of another's mind and his own, generally weaker, self-consciousness.
In this sense, he sees, however vaguely, differences in human
behavior, historically and sociologically defined, which are
neither a matter of birth nor social necessity but of "conscious"
and consistent choice. Again, the choice is submerged, not truly
self-conscious, because it is customary or, in other words, cultural.

While this is a simplified view of culture, it is appropriate for describing a hybrid cultural concept which strikingly
replicates the dilemma of the drunken driver. The drunken driver
does not recognize the extent to which his perception of reality
has been distorted. He knows from memory he can make reality--
i.e., his body and the car--conform to the road. When this illusion
is intruded upon by the unexpected accident, he will either
become more self-conscious, or, if drunk enough, he will assume
that reality, in particular the car, has gone haywire. His dilemma
is not so much that his senses are dulled by alcohol as it is
that he is not adequately self-conscious. It is this inadequacy
which marks the prevalent hybrid racial-cultural concept. It
is not accidental that this concept is typically explained in terms
which imply a dissonance between reality and perception (discussed
below). The concept is usually signified by the terms cultural
deprivation or cultural disadvantage.

As a cognitive process, cultural deprivation means that
the other race, blacks, lacks all, or part of, some "culture"
possessed by the white observer. Empirically, this cognition is
as close to the genetic cognition of race as it is to the broader
cultural one. The link to the genetic view is perhaps more fact-
ual than theoretical in that the holder of this concept, like the
drunk, could conceivably be more self-conscious. In fact, he
is not usually sufficiently aware to realize that cultural deprivation is a negative notion, and that it assumes knowledge of a
positive character in the culturally endowed. Since this latter
quality is not, or has not been, specified,*the observer general-
izes that all behavior unfamiliar to his group is culturally
unrealistic. Consequently, all behavior that is inconsistent with
his sub-conscious notion of reality is pathological; there is not
other American culture, only irrationality.

---

* Such specification, more common during slavery, existed along-
  side of pejorative genetic views of race, and usually fabricated
  notions of African barbarism.

Ultimately, the aspect of negation in the one-sided cultural concept indicates that it is a mediated form of seeing race; it is more a product of sophistication and of analyzing race than of simply perceiving it.* Of course, no view of race is completely unmediated; it is a matter of the degree to which one concept is sociologically automated. The presence of mediation becomes significant in the transition from "seeing race" to seeing it as a problem and as an object·for public policy.

Whenever Americans discuss racial public policy, the language stumbles over and through descriptions of alternatives along the conservative-liberal continuum. The alternatives are currently followed, with rare exception, by qualifications, not merely of degree, but of substantive description as well. The terms con-servative and liberal may be imperfect for the description of any area of public policy, but they are particularly so for racial questions. First, the correspondence between the conservative-liberal dimension in other policy areas and racial policy is generally very low. Secondly, the significance of particular goals fluctuates so frequently that they cannot be classified as liberal or conservative except by the reputations of their supporters. Thirdly, and perhaps most significantly there are enormous differences within the liberal or conservative groups in relation to the race issue. Black political behavior, has to be classified as entirely liberal, but this classification covers a host of conflicts, perhaps as difficult to resolve as differences between the two extremes of the conservative-liberal dimension. Similarly, contradictory policies have been found to emanate from people who are equally receptive or equally hostile to the other racial group. What has not generally be adequately recognized is that norms or attitudes about race can be indicative of a specific policy orientation only·in conjunction with one of the limited forms of cognition which characterize American policy perspectives in this area.

By cross-tabulating cognition of race and explicit values or tactics one can identify the policy orientation and direction of ideological groups in general social systems terms. This is the purpose of the following chart.

---

* However, this does not limit its applicability to our model
of the cognitive process because, by all but the most narrowly
positivistic phenomenological and epistemological standards
the same can be said, though to a lesser degree, of the other
two forms of cognition.

Table I

Tactic or Value Expressed ↓	Race → Physiological Concept	Cultural Concept
Integration	Complete Integration: Racial Assimilation, i.e. Participation in established two-party system, and interest groups. Non-negotiable.	Ethnic pluralism Secondary group integration. Primary group separation: i.e., limited black electoral participation Interracial colitions likely.
Separation	Complete Racial Separation of all institutions and territory. Non-negotiable. (Violence is likely.)	Expedient secondary group integration Political Action is mostly non-electoral. Territoral separation is unlikely.

11

The most evident cognitive position on race in American history is "genetic". This position holds simply that race consists of a set of hereditary biological characteristics. It is at this level that the most popular understanding of the Garvey movement and some white segregationist groups come together in terms of policy, because cognitively there is no statement of good or bad, superiority or inferiority. This cognitive orientation toward race has historically been accompanied by various normative orientations. This is to say, a segregationist who conceives of race as a genetic phenomenon is in full normative flower when he believes that the white race is irrevocably superior to the black one. He may believe that this qualitative difference too resides in the brain, spine, or feet, for that matter, but the important thing for him is the irrevocability of the difference. Similarly, we may find a black nationalist of the same cognitive bent, but of course, with the opposite normative interpretation of superiority. On the other hand, one can hold this same cognitive position and yet be an integrationist. This implies that one views genetic differences normlessly or rather that one believes such differences exist but have no social significance. Segregationist, as well as nationalist, policies would continually go against the grain of such a person. It is, of course, imaginable that he could behave in the most racially biased manner, but to do so while perceiving race as a neutral phenomenon would render him painfully conscious of his deliberate self-denial and self-rejection. The causes of this limited possibility, moreover, would reside in social or economic forces and not in personal choice. Needless to say, policy and even personal choice may well be a result of social and economic forces, but it is not likely that personal or individual group policy choices are made in clear and direct contradiction to the individual consciousness.

It should be obvious that the three aforementioned policy positions do not adequately depict the major orientations toward race in American politics. What may not yet be obvious is that the policy alternatives on race are thus exhausted as long as race is genetically conceived. Implicit in the racial programs which fall outside these policy descriptions are other cognitive orientations toward race, which will be explicated and compared later. In the process of analysis we will assume that there are only three kinds of normative orientations with which genetic cognitions may combine in creating policy: prejudice, racial neutrality, and nationalism. For the present, we need not define these familiar terms, except to say that prejudice denotes one's hatred of another racial group, neutrality denotes indifference to racial identity, and nationalism denotes an overriding interest in the advance of one's own race. When these three kinds of norms combine with various cognitions of race, the policy permutations

12

which they can produce are both numerous and, at the present level
of political science, unpredictable. We have tended to think,
for example, that racial neutrality always leads to integration,
but historically this has not been the case. In fact, if we look
at race relations merely in terms of norms, history holds too
many exceptions for scientific prediction. Social science itself
has been dominated by a functionalist view of society and a
definition of the race problem as one of integration and assimilation of minorities into the mainstream of a consensus-based
society.[14] No doubt, the development of cognitive and normative
values is bound up in an individual psychological process, which
complicates prediction. Yet, we propose that much of the development of these values occurs in predictable social group patterns
which are called cultural and racial. Accordingly Karl Deutsch
observes, "consciousness in a group or nation is far more primitive
[than individual consciousness] , and far more accessible to
observation and analysis."[15]

   Policy formation, like educational interaction, does not
occur in a vacuum. Most often true education--defined as the
development of self-consciousness--takes place in the larger world
and is not the "normal" function of the school. Governmental
actions, often devoid of substantive content, acquire a symbolic
meaning--mediated by a cultural apparatus--that shape our cognitions
in different ways. Busing as educational policy, for example,
is merely a physical technique that is only indirectly related
to educational development. As a symbol, however, busing has
influenced cognitions in various ways. Both blacks and whites
have become preoccupied with forms rather than content--the
menu is left untouched.

   Until all of us reach a stage of racial self-consciousness,
educational policy will never be racially neutral. In terms of
our concepts of race and expressed values we may identify four
orientations toward policy. Yet, for any one individual or
group these orientations are in a constant state of flux.[16]
In the area of religion, for example, blacks were forced to
create separate institutions (e.g., Richard Allen, Absalom Jones).
As time passed and social conditions changed, blacks were free
to attend many white churches; but most chose to remain apart.
Over the last decade black theologians have developed a black
theology which assigns a unique and positive role to these racial
institutions created under negative conditions. Black education
holds even greater promise for bringing about a reconciliation
of the nationalist-integrationist conflict and broadening the
cultural horizons of the United States. But a black educational
philosophy, with universal utility, has not been developed,
largely due to the obstacles discussed in the following chapters.

13

[1]Langston Hughes and Arna Bontemps (eds.) Book of Negro Folklore (N.Y.: Dodd, Mead and Company, 1958) p. 508.

[2]Martin Carnoy Education as Cultural Imperialism (N.Y.: McKay, 1974) pp. 234-235.

[3]Raymond Wolters The New Negro on Campus (Princeton, N.J.: Princeton University Press, 1975) p. 10.

[4]Carnoy, Education as Cultural Imperialism, p. 289.

[5]Philip Hauser quoted in Bennett Harrison Education, Training, and the Urban Ghetto (Baltimore: Johns Hopkins University Press, 1972) p. 9. One assumes that "Americanization" means cultural assimilation.

[6]Herbert Gintis quoted in Harrison, Education, Training, and the Urban Ghetto, p. 129.

[7]Milton Gordon Assimilation in American Life (N.Y.: Oxford University Press, 1964) p. 37.

[8]John Oliver Killens And Then We Heard Thunder

[9]Pierre L. van den Berghe Race and Racism (N.Y.: Wiley & Sons, 1967) p. 9.

[10]Ibid., pp. 9-10.

[11]George Simpson and J. Milton Yinger Racial and Cultural Minorities (N.Y.: Harper and Row, 1953) p. 46.

[12]Oliver C. Cox Caste, Class and Race (N.Y.: Modern Reader, 1948. p. 393.

[13]Simpson and Yinger, Racial and Cultural Minorities, p.12.

[14]Van den Berghe, Race and Racism, p.7.

[15]Karl Deutsch Nationalism and Social Communication (N.Y.: 1953.

[16]The instability of racial cognitions may be viewed from a number of perspectives. In his modernization approach to race relations, Pierre L. van den Berghe sees the existing degree of conflict as one of the basic dimensions in which

14

[16]the paternalistic type of race relations differs from the
competitive one and the instability and change typical of
the competitive type result in large measure from the dialectic
of conflict between subordinate and dominant groups. (Race and
Racism, p. 36). Wilson Carey McWilliams views fraternity as
existing only in a state of tension, incompleteness, and
ambivalence. Alienated from society, men are still in society
and are bound to it by lesser loyalty. Fraternity is made
both necessary and possible by that tension, providing the
only world in which man is free from divided loyalty, in which
there is a genuine alliance between emotion and vision. (The
Idea of Fraternity in America, p. 29). Thus true racial self-
consciousness does not guarantee an absence of tension nor
does it promote stability. Yet it does enable men to live
as equals and allies.

CHAPTER II

The Ideological Framework of
Political Choice on Racial Issues:
Nationalism and Integrationism in Education.........

Behind the veil dividing the American racial groups, of which
W.E.B. DuBois often spoke, there is an entire black social community.[1] In conversation discontinuous spheres in American life-
styles are commonly recognized; note, for example, the use of
soul as applied to black people. Yet social scientists have as
a rule rejected the concept of soul, in a priori way, or have at
least denied it any theoretical significance. One may say it is
too vague or meaningless a term ever to be elevated to the level
of "scientific" precision. Yet, we must deal with what it could
mean, in the absence of more precise substitutes. The term
suggests a distinctive style of life behind the veil, a distinctive set of values, norms, and behavior patterns. It implies
distinctiveness on all levels, including political culture and
behavior. Distinctive from what? It is a separation which asserts
the development of racial groups in ways which reflect their diverse
experience. Thus DuBois finds that there are "souls" of black
and white folks.[2] Political scientists, among others, may have
the right to conclude, but not to assume, a universal continuity
in American political structure and style. However, if a fundamental difference exists between black and white groups, it will
have a determining effect on the politics of either group, both
theoretically and empirically. For the present we cannot attempt
to resolve the issue, but we can make some empirical observations
about black politics in an effort to develop a theory of the
political significance of "being black."

Prevading all descriptions of black political action in
America are notions variously referred to as social change, reform,
revolution, and liberation. Certainly not all black political
action has led to social change, nor has all of it been appropriately
structured to do so, but virtually all of it has laid claim to
this kind of goal. It seems obvious that no politically signi-

ficant black groups or persons would admit to seeking the perpetuation of their subservient social status, a status which in fact
denies them a chance to seek much of anything. Yet, it is important to distinguish between goals and effects, between intention
and actuality, because our judgment of individual actors will
vary according to our emphasis,

As with uniformity of goal orientations, there is a basic
similarity in the consequence-oriented descriptions of black
political movements; that is, none of them have succeeded in creating an unoppressive social order. Thus we arrive at the rather
simplistic conclusion that none of these political actors have
achieved what they sought. In order to get beyond this general-
ization we must separate a political action from its effect.
Our understanding will, of course, be incomplete until the uncertain relationship between the two is clarified. However, DuBois'
exposition of black political goals is an excellent beginning
for this kind of analysis.

In the general realm of American political thought, social
change as a goal holds a comparatively prominent position. In
the common sense and often in the political scientists's sense of
ideology, all ideologies are presumed to fall somewhere within
or between conservatism and liberalism.[3] Defining ideology, for
the present, as a coherent set (logically or psychologically)
of orientations toward action, we can place individual political
goals in a confining and meaningful context. The ideological
context, however, can have more or less relevance to black politics
depending on the definition of its cognitive (object referent)
aspect. Where the conservatism-liberalism distinction is given
the broadest interpretation, namely support for the status quo
in America against advocacy of societal change, there is some
theoretical significance for black politics. The significance
is, however, rather low because it leaves the whole of black
politics on one side, the liberal side. When the distinction
has been made more specific in terms of political objects which
cut across the America polity, it has become almost irrelevant
to black politics. The cognitive content along which conservatives and liberals separate, as seen by Philip Converse, for
example in civil rights, can hardly be viewed from DuBois' perspective as a primary issue along which black political action
proceeds.

In an attempt to measure social class differences in ideology,
Converse argues that elite beliefs are more "constrained"--that
is, coherent and unified--than mass public beliefs. Seeking
evidence for this variation of beliefs, he uses the following
survey questions.

17

1. Negroes should be kept out of professional athletics.

2. The government should see to it that Negroes get fair treatment in jobs and housing.

3. The government should give federal aid only to schools that permit Negroes to attend.[4]

There is a definite ethnocentric illogic to using these questions as a test for ideology across racial groups. The illogic resides in the failure to account for cognitive differences which should be reasonably assumed to result from the unique identities and histories of black and white Americans. In the first question Negroes are not to Negroes the same as Negroes are to whites--that is, Negroes can only be an "other" for whites and not for themselves. Thus, when this question is asked, its effect on blacks, as opposed to their "other" is closer to: "People should be kept out of professional athletics." The cognitive fault is not simply in the word referents themselves but in the way the change affects the emphasis of the question. With the original question, Converse assumes that he is tapping "sympathy" toward Negroes. In the second form the question focuses on the right or power to keep people out. Thus, the relative significance of the question within any American ideology becomes indeterminant. The whole questionnaire presupposes that the ideological universe with respect to Negroes is bound by "integration" and segregation. While this was probably true for whites in 1956, it excluded an important variable for blacks, namely nationalism. Both nationalist and integrationist might give the negative answer to the question and then again they might not. Consider the nationalist followers of Marcus Garvey who accepted "white only" groups, and yet were apparently sympathetic toward Negroes.

The second and third questions seem to divide the sympathetic and the non-sympathetic, but there is reason to doubt that they do any more than simple division. Whites merely sympathetic toward blacks may well find this question more ideologically central than those who are empathetic or blacks themselves. For the latter, there is historically much less reason to believe "the government" or the federal government is an unbiased protector. It looks more or less biased depending on the direction of one's own bias. The logical extension of this problem to questions about foreign aid or social welfare policy, which were used by Converse and others, is that they suffer still from the orientation bias.

The implication of this observation is that the general conservative and liberal categories, defined by their content, obscure the black part of the American ideological universe. What

then takes the place of this distinction in black politics? The
answer is problematic, first because we are not decided upon the
object content of the liberal-conservative dimension, and secondly
because we are uncertain of the ideological status of the distinction.[5] Assuming a more particularistic content of the kind just
mentioned, the nationalist-integrationist distinction can be seen
as its black counterpart. Allowing, on the other hand, for the
broadest interpretation, it is still better to conclude that conservatism and liberalism are no more significant across racial groups
than are the number of individuals who have crossed this line.
Rather, as DuBois suggests, nationalism and integrationism are
decidedly more pertinent in characterizing black politics.

    This is not to suggest that they are tenets of fundamentally
divergent ideologies. On the contrary, it will be hypothesized
that nationalism and integrationism are secondary divergences of
goals within a larger coherent unit of beliefs. By DuBois'
analysis they are secondary tenets and political goals within a
coherent ideology of black liberation. The inclusiveness of
that analysis, and the ideology, "DuBoisism," thus implied is the
concern of this chapter.

    Looking back on the history of black politics in the United
States, DuBois saw a cycle of political movements against racial
oppression which were never able to relieve that oppression but
seemed merely to shift back and forth in their attacks on it.
Except, perhaps, for the struggle against slavery, this continuing
cycle can be cast in terms of nationalism and integrationism.
In this connection, DuBois observes:

> The bright ideals of the past—physical
> freedom, political (electoral) power,
> the training of brains and the training
> of hands,—all these in turn have waxed
> and waned, until even the last grows
> dim and overcast. Are they all wrong—
> all false? No, not that, but each alone
> was oversimple and incomplete,—the
> dreams of a credulous race-childhood,
> or the fond imaginings of the other
> world which does not know and does not
> want to know our power. To be really
> true all these ideals must be melted
> and welded into one.[6]

    Thus DuBois indicates his aim of healing a split in black
politics which nevertheless remains seventy years later. Yet his
evaluation of the controversy has had an indelible effect on the
way it has since proceeded. He was, moreover, successful on the

on the level of political thought in welding the ideals into one.

What does this welding together mean? Allowing for simpli-
fication, it entails giving a single, unifying meaning to diverse
black expressions; it means placing these expressions in a single
theoretical framework; it means, in some sense, putting forth
a cultural philosophy relevant to politics.[7] To a considerable
extent, this was not a creative process, because DuBois was not
solely writing a normative philosophy; he was not just attempting
to say what Black people should be doing or had failed to do.
He was largely engaged in a social and political analysis of black
history to determine what had been done, what was being done, and
what was continuous in those things called political action.
What he sought to create was a theoretical structure containing
analytic concepts adequate to bridge the gaps between moves toward
civil rights, economic rights and accomodationist segregation,
and to find a meaningful whole.

However successful he may have been in drawing together these
diverse ideological strains, it was primarily for his own intellectual satisfaction. Black activists and intellectuals have
been impressed by his well reasoned and often moving appeals for
ideological unity, but for the most part, they seem to have been
unconvinced. There has been no large scale, organizational
response among blacks, generating a flexible approach to problems
of integration and nationalism. None, that is, with the possible
exception of organized approaches to public education.

The politics of education was at once the most likely problem
area in which clear, consistent policy formulation would be needed
and sought, and the area in which black originated policy alternatives would meet the clearest resistance. Next to the maintenance
of slavery, the regulation and restriction of educational opportunity
has been the most sacred principle of social and racial oppression.
It is largely through the restriction of education that the in-
cessant recourse to claims of genetic inferiority has retained
its air of legitimacy and objectivity. As social scientists
such as Samuel Bowles have argued, the maintaince of presumably
more fundamental economic inequalities has hinged on their reinforcement through educational inequities.[8]

It is understandable then that black nationalists, for all
their tenacity, have rarely ever articulated a concise policy
for nationalistic education. When they have pursued all-black
education, it has always been, as with the Nation of Islam, an
additive on "integrated" education. The integrationists, however,
seem to have been more successful in the light of the Federal
government response to the Civil Rights movement. Yet, this

20

response may be no more than appearance because federally defined
school integration is quite unlike their own goals. In particular, black integrationists have yet to renounce, as a whole,
unenforced racial separation in education; the black college provides an example. Moreover, the black demand for school integration has been articulated more consistently as a right denied
than as a value not to be questioned.

The systematic restriction of educational access to blacks,
less than any other legal-social restriction, had generated
little debate and less recourse to judicial apology among whites
before 1954. From the earliest efforts by blacks to gain educational access, its denial was argued on the basis of intellectual
standards and native ability. The de jure right itself was
denied to blacks during slavery, but whites behaved, for the
most part, as if this denial was merely secondary to the presumed
ineducability of blacks. Accordingly, early black leaders, who
were generally well educated, were treated as the exceptions which
proved the rule. Repression in this area did not seem to require
the vigorous defenses made in other areas of segregation because,
though few realized it, educational barriers drew strength from
the environment of more rigidly enforced repression.

When blacks individually penetrated this barrier during
slavery, they were likely to become political leaders. Frederick
Douglass, for one, had done so through informal education and
training while another, Martin Delany, had acquired an extensive
formal education. Yet, as leaders, the first called integrationist
and the second a nationalist, they were never able to provide
strong leadership on the question of education.

II.   Ideological Development in Black Politics

DOUGLASS OR DELANY: POLITICS AND BELIEFS

The bright ideals of the black political past could already
be characterized in terms of nationalist and integrationist
controversy when DuBois rose to prominence. With his rise the
controversy reached full development; he fell forcefully into the
fight; he described the controversy and analyzed it; and finally
withdrew from it (or rose above it).

The ideological dichotomy could be seen developing before
the end of slavery in the disagreement between Frederick Douglass
and Martin Delany. Douglass made a vivid allusion to this dichotomy
when he said, "I thank God for making me a man simply, but Delany
always thanks Him for making him a black man." Historical references to Douglass and Delany incline us to stereotype the former

21

as an integrationist and the latter as a nationalist,[9] but this
view is distorted by the fact that these concepts belong to a
later period in black political history which they were in the
process of creating. Like so many original men, they can only
loosely be identified with their followers. In subsequent
generations, using Douglass's metaphor "to be a man simply,"
integration, like nationalism, embodies widely divergent concepts
and attitudes.

It is impossible to say whether Douglass would have sought
to integrate, if he had not lived in a time in which next to
nothing was even tokenly integrated. Both he and Delany lived
in slavery and fought for its elimination as their first priority.
Beyond this "physical freedom," the only particular demand which
loomed large in Douglass's career was the integration of the
American electoral process. The rights to vote and hold political
office have been sufficient goals to categorize him as an integrationist. Yet, in later years, we have seen that integration includes
racial mixing in numerous social, economic and political areas
beyond elections.

Delany's individual and organizational interests never came
into direct conflict with Douglass, and yet they were contemporaries
leading blacks in different directions. Perhaps, the presence of
slavery, as an agreed upon evil, shaped their vision of the good
society in a compatible way. Certainly, as indicated by Delany's
later years, he was not adamantly opposed to electoral integration.
Still, he devoted most of his politically active years to a nationalistic separation of blacks and whites.

At first Delany saw South America as a place to which slaves
might move in order to gain freedom from slavery. Later, he joined
with the African Colonization Society in proposing Africa, particularly the Congo, as the place to which American blacks might go.
Behind his emphasis on migration to Africa was a relatively broad
belief in black American character and culture which constituted
a basis for independent social organization. Migration was not
seen merely as a tactical necessity for blacks escaping slavery
but as a good for all blacks, although only a few would be capable
of going. In almost a name-by-name review of freedmen, Delany
sought to enumerate the occupational skills, education, and social
values which could provide a basis for independent black social
organization.[10] Obviously, a prime category in the establishment
of his good society, judging from his writings, included the
socially useful skills of its citizens. However, the extent to
which this society constituted a distinct ideological departure
from the slavery-capitalist system of his background is only
clear with regard to slavery.

Delany, as Douglass recognized, sought to emphasize the
beauty and, to some extent, the superiority of blacks in America.
This theme he surely bequeathed to later black nationalists. Yet,
involved in the value of superiority is an objective content which
is not immune to, nor exclusive of, integrationism. Black superiority might have resided in the concrete achievements of blacks
in American society for Delany. In this respect, slaves survived
and freed blacks prospered in spite of adverse conditions. More
likely, however, Delany's notions of superiority rested in a
belief that blacks had a superior system of values and orientation
toward social organization developed over time. Thus, he seems
to have maintained, more implicitly than explicitly, a notion
of black culture. Such a belief is not excluded by integrationists,
but is more apparent among the group called "cultural nationalists."

        In the designation of their political objectives, the two men
created two distinct views of the black American society which
should follow emancipation. They were not, however, sufficiently
explicit in the expression of social alternatives, nor sufficiently
thorough in their criticism of the American social order to have
originated distinct ideologies. Douglass did not accept Delany's
"characteristic" political behavior and Delany for a time, did
not support Douglass's programs. These simple behavioral differences cannot be considered ideological in content, unless they
occur with the consistent inclusion or exclusion of several kinds
of political acts, all of which focus on some conscious value.

        An important verification of the basic consensus between the
two men emerges from their critique, or lack of it, of educational
alternatives. It is quite understandable that neither of them
sought educational integration given the apparent hopelessness of
such a proposal at any time before the turn of the century. In
particular, both men had had to fight during slavery for the right
to any formal education at all. The result was that Delany received
a medical degree from Harvard University before the Civil War while
Douglass followed, with exceptional success, the path of informal
self-education--a path to which most educated blacks were forced
to resign themselves.[11]

        If emancipation had not been the primary preoccupation of both
men, it is still unlikely that they would have fundamentally
disagreed over education. Education was seen by both as a means
of developing black leadership through the acquisition of skills.
As such, it was believed that the needed skills should be equal to
the potential tasks, and not necessarily equal to that of whites.
In other words, the importance of education among white Americans
had not reached the level of intensity and structure requisite
for it to function well as a means of status-quo maintenance.

For the black nationalist social inequality was sufficiently
salient to allow for the persistence of nationalist thought among
those educated in integrated institutions. For the integrationist
segregated education was certainly preferable to none at all,
and probably more desirable at the time than integrated education.

Of course, Delany's hopes for emigration would seem to negate
any possibility for integrated education, but the possibility
remains because Delany did not expect complete emigration.
Moreover, to the extent that we are concerned with ideology and
ideological continuity among nationalists, it is important to
examine Delany's earlier and later years, when he substantially
abandoned the idea of emigration. In this regard, two factors
seem crucial. First, Delany's recourse to emigration pivoted
on his critique of whites as concretely and self-consciously racist
and discriminatory. Racial differences were, as he understood
them, both cultural and physical.[12] Given this combination, he
anticipated an extended competition between blacks and whites
in which one would enjoy superordination as long as possible.
The competition would take on an overt character of violent coercion
and economic exploitation. He had no profound concept of cultural
bias in education, and consequently very little reason to believe
that if whites were to concede to integration in education blacks
would suffer by accepting it.

Nevertheless, there are elements of a cultural concept in
Delany's speeches. He says, for example, "that the colored races
have the highest traits of civilization will not be disputed."[13]
From this perspective he could not have expected that integration
would be wholly beneficial for black education, but there remained
room for flexibility. In the long run, he may have sharpened his
belief in racial-cultural distance. In the short run, however,
he succumbed to a view of blacks as "peaceable" and therefore
unlikely to sustain nationalist organization. In the words of
historian Sterling Stuckey, he illustrated "a black nationalist
tendency to exaggerate the degree of acquiescence to oppression
by the masses of black people."[14]

DuBOIS - WASHINGTON CONFLICT

The issues in the conflict between DuBois and Booker T.
Washington were not clearly drawn; they both stood on the same
side of many American intellectual fences. Both of them saw and
disdained the subordinate status which blacks had been assigned,
but differed in their approaches to raising this status. Although
it is difficult to tell what Washington's primary ideological
commitment was, it is feasible that he could have maintained the
same fundamental values as DuBois and still have pursued his own

24

policy without apparent contradiction. Their conflict can be
seen as purely tactical. Using simple behavior as a measure of
values, Washington did very little in terms of policy that DuBois
wanted to oppose, but much of what he said, DuBois had to reject.
There was, however, some difference of opinion which cannot easily
be relegated to the tactical level. Still this difference was
secondary in that it did not involve the central aspects of their
views.

     The one tactical difference between them involves the often
criticized part of "Booker T'ism" known as "accommodation."
Washington gave lucid expression to the accommodationist viewpoint
in his influential Atlanta Exposition Address of 1895, where he
gratified an expectant white audience by saying, "In all things
that are purely social we can be as separate as the fingers,
yet one as the hand in all things essential to mutal progress."[15]
Thus, Washington was accommodating the Southern as well as the
American majorities, whose apparent feelings were echoed a year
later from the apex of American jurisprudence in the case of
"Plessy v. Ferguson" with the euphemism of separate but equal.

     The effect of Washington's accommodationism seems to have
been to reinforce separate and very unequal interracial relations,
but these consequences were unintentional. Exemplary evidence of
a contrary intention is provided by his public opposition to black
disenfranchisement in Louisiana. [16] An indication of tactical
possibilities which Washington saw in accommodation is found in
his characteristically cautious method of prodding Southern
whites to change their ways. In its potential for reducing the
violence blacks suffered from whites, the following remark may
have been more effective than direct protest:

          Another danger in the South, which should be
          guarded against, is that the whole white South,
          including the wise, conservative, law-abiding
          element, may find itself represented before the
          bar of public opinion by the mob, or lawless
          element, which gives expression to its feelings
          and tendency in a manner that advertises the
          South throughout the world. Too often those who
          have no sympathy with such disregard of law are
          either silent or fail to speak in a sufficiently
          emphatic manner to offset, in any large degree, the
          unfortunate reputation which the lawless have
          too often made for many portions of the South.[17]

The success that can be claimed, though not statistically demonstrated, for the accommodationist approach to interracial violence cannot be carried much farther. Bodily violence is not the only or principal means of suppression, nor the most convenient because it can easily induce violent reaction. Consequently, the more sophisticated conservatives would have reason to want it confined. In fact Washington's proposal for "mutal progress" involves a certain interracial compatibility. This compatibility could hardly have meant primary group level integration, but beyond this level of separation, accommodation, dedicated to mutual progress, loses its identity. If it meant separation on the secondary level, and it clearly did mean that in the case of educational institutions, then it smacks of nationalism (though it was not, in DuBois' terms). It coincides with the simplistic and most readily apparent characteristic of nationalism, racial independence. That this independence could not be realized is only an indictment of the analytical component of his thought and not its intentional aspect.

The confusion is reduced, though not overcome, by looking at the second aspect of Booker T'ism capsulized by a statement in the Atlanta address, "Cast down your buckets where you are."[18] The statement is an explication of his mutual progress notion. It connects accommodation with a normative or goal-oriented assertion which is otherwise lacking. Casting down your bucket is a virtue in itself, but accommodation is simply expedient to a higher purpose.

Washington asked both blacks and whites to cast down their buckets but the meaning for each group was quite different. He wanted whites to dig into the black labor supply and he wanted blacks to develop their own skills and businesses. Harold Cruse calls the latter aim "Black Capitalism" and in turn identifies this as economic nationalism;[19] however, the relationship is rather hazy. To avoid such a premature conclusion, this notion can be referred to as "the ginger-cake commitment." The name derives from a story Washington tells of his childhood in slavery. He saw two white mistresses eating ginger-cake on the terrace of the big house and he commented that he would have everything he wanted when he was in a position to eat ginger-cake like that.[20]

While man does not live by eating ginger cakes alone, man has often rated the attainment of materialistic ends very high. The ginger-cake commitment is a capitalistic orientation toward the best life, but it is more adequately described by the term materialism. However vague the definitions of capitalism may be, they must include free and private ownership of land and means of production, and the ginger-cake commitment does not seem to go this far. Since blacks were expected to develop

26

mechanical and industrial skills which would make them desirable employees of non-black businesses, there is a certain lack of concern with ownership. Thus Washington asked wealthy whites to cast their buckets down among skilled blacks. Unfortunately his accommodationists skills were the only ones scooped up.

Perhaps, the ginger-cake commitment taken alone can be identified with black capitalism, but in conjunction with the white-directed part of the economics program, the identity falls apart. Moreover, when accommodationism is added to this, we see that Booker T'ism contradicts the notion of ownership. Black economic independence means the loss of white superordination and also suggests economic redistribution, both of which are antithetical to the notion of social stability implicit in accommodation. If Booker T'ism is to be called black capitalism, as Cruse proposes, then we must conclude that both lack an essential element of capitalism (a possibility).

The apparent contradiction between the ginger-cake commitment and the rest of Booker T'ism must be superseded in the central concept of the ideology. An ideology, as used here, must be characterized by an overriding principle in which none of the particular beliefs encompassed are contradicted. Having found contradiction at this level we are led to assume the presence of a higher ideological plane. Yet, there is none apparent in Washington's expressions. The assumption does not imply a conscious, but secret, awareness of a more primary commitment on Washington's part. Rather, it means that if Washington's thought is to be understood as ideology, coherence must be assumed, even if it is unconscious.[21]

DuBois' criticism of Booker T'ism is that Washington did not understand the meaning of his own program, and therefore behaved illogically and inconsistently with respect to goals which DuBois never rejected. Considering DuBois' socialist orientation, he might have attacked Washington's ginger-cake commitment on a normative level. Yet that he did not do so is immediately understandable because he did not show this socialist inclination until several years after his critique of Washington.

DuBois' critique of Booker T'ism consisted of three main points which come out in the article, "Of Mr. Booker T. Washington and Others,"[22] points which, as we shall see, bear importantly on our understanding of the place of nationalism and integrationism in DuBois' philosophy.[23] In this article DuBois also attacks Washington's claim to black leadership and the power of the Tuskegee Machine. This point of view, which will not be given detailed discussion here, is illustrated in the following DuBois quote.

27

If the best of American Negroes receive by outer
pressure a leader whom they had not recognized
before, manifestly there is here a certain palpable
gain. Yet, there is also irreparable loss,--a
loss of that peculiarly valuable education which
a group receives when by search and criticism
it finds and commissions its own leaders. The
way in which this is done is at once the most
elementary and the nicest problem of social
growth. History is but the record of such group-
leadership; and yet how infinitely changeful is
its type and character! And of all types and
kinds, what can be more instructive than the
leadership of a group within a group?"[24]

For DuBois, Washington's leadership was artificial and consequently counter-productive because it was externally imposed on
blacks.

DuBois argues that accommodationism, which he refers to as
the "Atlanta Compromise" suffers from three major omissions. It
not only denigrates the right of blacks to full enfranchisement,
it also repudiates any form of political organization, by blacks,
intrasystemic or otherwise. Secondly, it gives support to a lega-
lized second-class citizenship in all areas even though it promotes
extra-legal changes. Thirdly, it leads to withdrawal of support
for black higher education. This is important to DuBois as an
avenue for the development of a critical black leadership.

The economic aspect of Booker T'ism also undergoes a tripartite
critique. This argument is directed more against the white-
oriented part of the casting down buckets notion, than against
the ginger-cake commitment, a refined version of which DuBois
accepted. First, a workingman's employment rights as well as his
property, business as well as personal, must be defended politically.
Secondly, the virtues of self-help are retained when a man has
self-respect. This self respect derives from a man's capacity
to assert himself in all areas of life, including political life.
Thirdly, the development of black economic skills and power depends
significantly on a compatible cultural development in which
liberally educated teachers, at Tuskegee for example, set the tone
and inspiration.[25]

DuBois brought the rather incoherent notions of Booker T'ism
together, and found contradictions. He did not reject everything
but instead identified Washington's "half-truths":

28

[T] he distinct impression left by Mr. Washington's propaganda is, first that the South is justified in its present attitude toward the Negro because of the Negro's degradation; secondly, that the prime cause of the Negro's failure to rise more quickly is his wrong education in the past; and thirdly, that his future rise depends primarily on his own efforts. Each of these propositions is a dangerous half-truth.[26]

The half of truth that he found was evidenced, particularly in later years, in DuBois' own thought, but he never recanted on Booker T'ism, as has been suggested.[27] The untruth was seen as Washington's failure to interrelate his program with a more theoretical social critique. In the first case, the degraded status of blacks must be explained by reference to white degrader. Secondly, it has not been the black man's failure to prepare himself for equality, in terms of skills, that has led to or perpetuated inequality. Thirdly and consequently, any change for blacks within the country's social system, including its economic subsystem, requires readjustment in all areas by both groups.

The rudiments of DuBois' understanding of nationalism and integrationism are present in Booker T'ism itself and were brought out by the conflict. There is a dualism in Booker T'ism between nationalism and integrationism, parallel to the "twoness" of DuBois; but in the former case the dualism is unresolved, even unrecognized. On the one hand, accommodation and being separate as the five fingers means a kind of nationalistically-based social system, that is to say, racial and cultural independence. On the other hand, it means accommodating a relationship of racial dependence, which is a form of integration. Similarly, the economic paradox meant blacks casting down their buckets among blacks, but at the same time it meant they should seek and prepare to fill white buckets. In contrast, DuBois' thought includes a mediation of these diverse tendencies.

ASPECTS OF DuBOIS' POLITICAL CRITIQUE: THE TALENTED TENTH

It is interesting that the article expounding the talented tenth idea came out about the same time as the article on Washington, and yet the former was published in a book edited by Washington.[28] It is significant because the idea was a first step beyond the thoughts expressed in the conflict. It is considered only an incomplete step because the notion of the talented tenth does not stand by itself; it does not clearly express his thought, and is easily confused.

29

The talented tenth concept has, perhaps, been confused with
the apologistic evaluations of the aristocracy, such as that of
Ortega y Gasset. However, DuBois' concept did not involve a leadership separated by wealth and leisure from the masses, as do the
aristocratic notions. Rather it involves a black leadership in
all areas of society, highly trained, culturally and technically,
and dedicated to black liberation. The notion is better criticized
for its idealism than its presumed aristocratic arrogance.[29]
The world of black leaders which DuBois saw could scarcely be
distinguished by wealth. DuBois, for example, never exerted much
effort to get beyond an income level very near poverty. [30]

DuBois makes a terse and eloquent call for the development
of the intellectually exceptional:

> The Negro race, like all races, is going to be
> saved by its exceptional men. The problem of
> education, then, among Negroes must first of all
> deal with the Talented Tenth; it is the problem
> of developing the Best of this race that they
> may guide the Mass away from the contamination
> and death of the Worst, in their own and other
> races. Now the training of men is a difficult
> and intricate task. Its technique is a matter
> for educational experts, but its object is for
> the vision of seers. If we make money the object
> of man-training, we shall develop money-makers
> but not necessarily men; if we make technical
> skill the object of education, we may possess
> artisans, but not, in nature, men. Men we shall
> have only as we make manhood the object of the
> work of the schools--intelligence, broad sympathy,
> knowledge of the world that was and is, and of
> the relation of men to it--this is the curriculum
> of the Higher Education which must underlie true
> life. On this foundation we may build bread winning,
> skill of hand and quickness of brain, with never
> a fear lest the child and man mistake the means
> of living for the object of living. [31]

Apparently, for DuBois, Washington had mistaken "the means
of living" for life itself; and he had likewise mistaken a method
of liberating blacks for the actual attainment of that liberation.
The argument does not fall into the disputable separation of means
and ends because one can assume that they are inseparable. The
rejoinder to that assumption, inferred here, is that without higher
education mere training is imcomplete and probably meaningless,
as a method or as a goal.

It is incomplete because specialized training must be integrated with other aspects of social life on the normative and cognitive levels. In terms of simple cognition, individuals understand what they do by defining their life in relationship to other things. In terms of values and norms, and ideological significance, DuBois sees a psychological necessity for a talented tenth, leaders who are expected to come from "centers of training where men are not so mystified and befuddled by the hard and necessary toil of earning a living, as to have no aims higher than their bellies, and no God greater than Gold."[32]

In another way DuBois saw this leadership as intrinsically bound to early socialization processes, and as essential to the stability of the black family. "Human education," he said, "is not simply a matter of schools; it is much more a matter of family and of one's social class. Now the black boy of the South moves in a black world—a world with its own leaders, its own thoughts, its own ideals."[33] This conclusion was no doubt supplemented by his comparatively rigorous sociological study of black community life.[34]

Unfortunately DuBois' exposition of the talented tenth is short on particularities or program. It is a general outline for part of a social organization; it sets out to describe a role, but it does not talk about recruitment and stabilization. The support of liberal arts education was important for recruitment but said little about implementation problems such as financing. He also skirted the problem of stabilizing an elite of virtue and avoiding its degeneration into an elite of wealth.

The substance of elite action was to consist fundamentally of a recognition and promotion of black culture. It was expected to define this culture on scholarly and common-sensical levels, and then to acquire authoritative leadership positions, by means of its superior knowledge, with which the masses could be guided through major political controversies, including nationalism and integrationism.

SOCIALISM IN BLACK

Socialism can be correlated with the talented tenth idea in that the former is expected to provide an antidote against abuses by the latter elite. That is to say, a socialistically organized society should not be conducive to status differentiation based on wealth. However, that the elite is not a socialistic elite, per se, is both theoretically and historically manifest. DuBois's socialist expression came years later, after he became editor of the NAACP's Crisis magazine in 1910. Thereafter his

31

socialism grew increasingly pronounced. In 1933 he argued "the reorganization of industry in this world for the benefit of those that work and not of those that buy and sell is certain."[35]

At no time was his socialism culturally disembodied; it always appeared in the form of black experience and values. While he argued that socialism is good for all, he consistently expounded its particular value to blacks. In an analytical fashion, he concluded that capitalism was conducive to, though not sufficient for, American racism. Conversely, socialism, he felt was conducive to, but insufficient, for black liberation.

DuBois argued that black culture should spawn its own version of socialist beliefs. He said: "The attempt to dominate Negro Americans by purely capitalistic ideas died with Booker T. Washington."[36] The fortunate failure of blacks to develop a capitalistic orientation was, he maintained, complimented empirically by the subservient and perhaps "non-economic status" of blacks. Namely, blacks lacked wealth, controlled nothing, and exploited even less--a conclusion that is more convincing in comparative than in absolute terms.

By the same token he resented the attempt of American Communists to subjugate the race to the class issue. He gave vent to this feeling in writing about the Scottsboro Cases in which communists supported the defense of several black youths who were being victimized by Southern racial injustice. He claimed that their disregard for racial problems led to unnecessary suffering by blacks in and out of courtrooms. As a sort of obiter dictum on the Communists' failure to help the defendants he added, "American Negroes do not propose to be the shock troops of the Communist Revolution...."[37]

In terms of social goals, DuBois argued as follows:

There exists today a chance for Negroes to organize a cooperative State within their own group.
By letting Negro farmers feed Negro artisans,
and Negro technicians guide Negro home industries,
and Negro thinkers plan this integration of
cooperation, while Negro artists dramatize and
beautify the struggle, economic independence
can be achieved. To doubt that this is possible
is to doubt the essential humanity and the equality
of brains of the American Negro."[38]

Thus, on both analytical and normative levels he saw blacks and whites moving along different paths of economic organization. He could not, therefore, take a position on the nationlist-integration issue which clearly contradicted this conclusion. What

32

is compatible is, first, a prior commitment to black interests and, second, a decision on nationalism-integrationism which would allow for the free expression of socialism among blacks.

There is perhaps some theoretical difficulty in reconciling emphases on class and race as major sources of social conflict. For Marx and his followers, one's class is determined by his relationship to the mode of production. This relationship determines his true consciousness and therefore his culture. Race and racism may be correlated with class, but the correlation is generally viewed as incidental. Thus, the problems of blacks are supposed to be the problems of poverty in an economic system that is not "actually racist" but "actually exploitive."[39] The implication is that an ideology which claims to be socialist must be purely so, and consequently there is no such thing as black socialism. In terms of long range goals, DuBois recognized that the interests of the poor were bound together. However, in terms of his commitment he was not sufficiently impressed by this argument to refrain from calling for socialism among blacks, first and before others.

The commitment to socialism can be expected to tend toward a commitment to integrated education because social class inequities are interracial, but such a tendency could only emerge in the long run, if at all, for several reasons. First, the appeal of social reorganization is primarily directed toward blacks. Secondly, the strength of the appeal is assumed to reside in the special evidence of black economic exploitation through racism. Thirdly, and perhaps most significant, is DuBois's belief, echoed by other blacks, that capitalism and its accompanying false consciousness have uniformly circumscribed conceptual frameworks of white Americans for decades to come.

Thus, the pursuit of socialism required some expectation of separate black training and education, at least at the higher educational levels. Since DuBois recognized in his argument for a talented tenth the importance of the formative years in developing a sound basis for social reorganization, the desirability of separate black elementary education could not be immediately restricted.

THE PRACTICE OF NATIONALISM-INTEGRATIONISM, DICHOTOMIZED

It has been indicated in the thoughts and political behavior thus far discussed that one's approach to the nationalist-integrationist distinction is invariably intertwined with one's position on these issues. The relationship seems to hold whatever one's definition of the distinction might be. It certainly holds under DuBois' definition. In order to understand that relationship and his definition of the concepts involved, we need to look first at his interpretation of these concepts on the "determinant" empirical level.

Characterizing this dualism as pervasive in black political history, Harold Cruse observes:

> The 'two difficult sets of facts,' DuBois refers to (Dusk of Dawn, p. 199) are integrationism (civil rights, racial equality, freedom) versus nationalism (separatism, accommodationist self-segregation, economic nationalism, group solidarity and self-help). This was truly the first theoretical formulation of the historical conflict between tendencies... 40

It is easy to accept Cruse's deference to DuBois in this regard, but it is not so easy to accept what Cruse brackets as exemplifying the dualistic tendencies. In fact, it is this kind of disagreement which plagued DuBois' relationship with other NAACP staff members.

Membership in the NAACP has come to mean, axiomatically, membership in an integrationist group. Its leadership, including White and Spingarn, opposed, in their words, "segregation in any form," but DuBois dissented. He argued first that the NAACP could not and should not oppose all segregation, particularly black self-segregation. He incurred the wrath of the organization leadership by arguing that the NAACP had never been opposed to self-segregation. They retaliated by forcing him out of the NAACP and by attempting to universalize their integrationism.

In the following statement by DuBois it seems evident that his reference to self-segregation is also a reference to nationalism:

> The opposition to segregation is an opposition to discrimination. The experience in the United States has been that usually when there is racial segregation, there is also racial discrimination. But the two do not necessarily go together, and there should never be an opposition to segregation pure and simple unless that segregation does involve discrimination... The same way in schools, there is no objection to schools attended by colored pupils and taught by colored teachers. On the contrary, colored pupils can by our own contention be as fine human beings as any other sort of children, and we certainly know that there are no teachers better than trained colored

teachers. But if existence of such a school
is made reason and cause for giving it worse
housing, poorer facilities, poorer equipment
and poorer teachers, then we do object, and
the objection is not against the color of the
pupils' or teachers' skins, but against the
discrimination. [41]

Here we see that DuBois advocates both sides of the "ism"
distinction, depending on the relevant circumstances. The principle which determines how he evaluates circumstances is not yet
made explicit. In contrast, there appears to be an open and clear
principle determining governmental action on more recent segregation issues. That is, the desegregation laws and court interpretations must be pursued, without regard to the question of discrimination in the racially unbalanced institution in question. The
continuing debate centers largely around how randomly or unre-
lentingly the problem is pursued. The present government is
untouched by or unconcerned with DuBois' argument that racial
separation has variable significance. With this argument in mind,
we are compelled to question the values implicit in governmental
policy which lead to a unilateral approach to racial separation
(segregation).

Such is the case with the 1970's conflict over "busing,"
where the conflict has centered around the degree of physically-
defined racial integration. Particularly in the North, whites
have grown increasingly opposed to busing while federal officials
and the courts have been publicly committed to it. With important
exceptions like the NAACP, blacks seem to be only lukewarmly
positive; that is, the vigor with which de jure integration was
pursued in the 1960's is no longer evident in the 1970's busing
conflict. While this decline in black activism may be explained
by a sense of satisfaction or by a sense of fatalism, the best
explanation emerges from the sense of alienation from the
(institutionalized) conflict itself. The real question for blacks
may well center on the power to integrate and the control of
education and not the resulting racial make-up itself. In this
case, modern blacks are close to DuBois who should not be characterized as an integrationist in the current sense without substantial
qualification.

Still, there are numerous instances other than his involvement
with the NAACP in which he behaved as would an integrationist.
Part of the argument he developed in the conflict with Washington,
that concerning political rights and electoral participation,
expressed integrationism. He carried this emphasis on electoral
participation to the point of asking blacks to gauge their support

of presidential candidates by their orientation to black voters.
The request that blacks choose between the two major parties is
one of the clearest cases of integration in DuBois' political
history.

He soon decided that the two party system was hopeless, and
therefore asked that black political integration be directed toward
the socialist party. While this is still racial integration, it
is much less so than two party politics. First, he thought the
socialists would give some representation to black interest, as
the two parties would never do. This he found more important
than the token representation offered by the system. [42]

Referring to electoral integration as "not so much wrong as
short-sighted," he argued "the democracy which we had been asking
for political life must sooner or later replace the tyranny which
now dominated industrial life."[43] He, therefore, supported
interracial labor solidarity and appealed, unsuccessfully, for
labor union integration. However, this appeal also came with
nationalistic qualifications. He observed in this respect:

> Negroes perceive clearly that the real interests
> of the white worker are identical with the interests
> of the black worker, but until the white worker
> recognizes this, the black worker is compelled
> in sheer self-defense to refuse to be made the
> sacrifical goat.[44]

To avoid further sacrifice, he suggested that black labor
should be self-organized. Similarly, he recognized the value of
separate black political organization. In advocating a black
political party, he said: "It is a move of segregation, it
'hyphenates' us, it separates us from our fellow Americans; but
self-defense knows no hesitations. The American Negro must
either vote as a unit or continue to be politically emasculated
as at present."[45]

Support of a black political party is significant national-
istically, although it is not so much so as other programs; it
still supposes integration in the electoral system. His emphasis
on black higher education, which grew out of the conflict with
Washington, is more reflective of nationalism. His agitation
for black-owned and controlled businesses has a similar quality.
Moreover, his argument that interracial violence, though undesir-
able, might be necessary, is indicative of nationalism. While
hoping to avoid violence, he said ". . . at the same time let us
set our faces grimly toward the fact, with unwinking eyes, that
it may be necessary. War is Hell, but there are things worse
than Hell, as every Negro knows."[46]

It should be apparent from these diverse examples of DuBois as a nationalist and as an integrationist that he was fundamentally neither of the two. These "isms" are for DuBois <u>tactical</u> considerations, that parallel the secondary importance conservatism and liberalism have to a more fundamental American creed, (for example, interest group liberalism).[47] These events indicate a unifying theoretical force and not, as Broderick claims, a split personality or indecisiveness.[48] Considering the iron-clad distinction made between the two, it is interesting to see how they come together in DuBois' ideology.

What is, however, more interesting is the implication of "DuBoisism" that they must be united. In fact, the primary concern of this discussion is to draw out the suggestion that one cannot reasonably be committed to either position as it has been described.[49]

MARCUS GARVEY: ANOTHER KIND OF NATIONALIST

It is also interesting in this connection to examine DuBois' rejection of Marcus Garvey's separatism, as against the alternative of Pan-Africanism. In spite of a bitter inter-personal exchange, DuBois observed that Garveyism added something of merit in black politics by building up "a racial ethos" and rejecting "attempts to escape from ourselves". However, DuBois rejected Garveyism because its notion of black culture was unrealistic and "fatuous". It sought to build racial pride but it did not take into account a cultural tradition and experience which needed more than "propaganda" to accomodate Garvey's plan.[50] DuBois felt that Pan-Africanism with its more limited goals rather than a "back to Africa program" was more in accord with the limits of the black experience in America.

The popular success of Garveyism would probably be underestimated if one counted only members of Garvey's official organization, the Universal Negro Improvement Association. Garvey claimed a following of 2 million in 1919, less than three years after he came to the United States from Jamaica. Eventually his estimate grew to about six million followers, but more conservative analysts have numbered his group in the range of a million plus.

The goal of the U.N.I.A. as expressed in the Constitution, written by Garvey himself, was "to establish a Universal Confraternity among the race; to promote the spirit of race pride and love; to reclaim the fallen of the race...." His motto was "One God, One Aim, One Destiny". In both statements one can see an emphasis on the unity of race and culture, but in the latter this unity is raised to the level of near absolute in which people

37

are differentiated in fundamental ways according to their race. This in itself does not make Garveyism an unrealistic or irrational ideology because culture does differentiate people in more or less fundamental ways--for example, in religions, language structure and leadership orientations. With perhaps some difference of degree, Garvey and DuBois come together in this belief.

Yet it is difficult to consider Garvey a cultural nationalist because the emphasis on culture was not central to his belief-system. Culture, for Garvey, was more a fact of black history which found a place in the structure and organizational procedure of his movement, than it was the object of his movement. This might be true of all nationalists but it can also be the case that cultural expression, development, or perpetuation are central to the goal-orientation and not just an accomplished fact. Garvey's Constitutional statement does not, then, well represent his ideology. It came to be characterized and pervaded by an emphasis on the physical separation of racial groups through black emigration.

The implementation of black culture in the Garvey movement, as opposed to ideology, is exemplified by its religious orientation. Offices and the political structure were defined in relation to divine and natural orders. Policies were likely to be justified first in terms of a moral order rather than as practical procedures. However, the particular character of the movement was not merely a reflection of the black religio-political tradition; the two may be quite distinct.[51] To that extent the movement did not embody the black culture, but it doubtlessly constituted a cultural variation by blacks from any American norm.

On the level of ideology, however, the central issues were physically-defined. There was no interest in bringing "valued-things" from the black American experience into the new society. There was virtually no assumption, for example, that the systems of economic organization and distribution would be any different in the future than in the past. By contrast, the fear of racial "mongrelization" received an excess of attention.[52] The central belief was that the natural order made it impossible for black-skinned people to live happily in the same nation-state with a white majority. Discounting the unsubstantial explanation of deliberate fraud by Garvey, it is clear that nearly all the money and the bulk of the energy of the organization were lost in the attempt to obtain African land and to transport American blacks there.

Garveyism was, then, a kind of weak cultural nationalism. More accurately it was a nationalism only concerned with changing the objective or rather physical conditions of a genetically-defined

38

racial group. A popular alternative characterization of black
ideologies is "revolutionary nationalism", but this is misleading
because revolution does not exclude an emphasis on black culture
and such an emphasis can be revolutionary. Revolution may well
come from the institutionalization of traditional values that
were previously not a significant part of the dominant, established institutions.

The limits of "revolutionary" nationalism, when deprived of
any cultural content, can be found in Garvey's failure to address
the question of formal education for black nationalists. While
he repeatedly appealed to his following to develop a strong black
consciousness and perspective, he failed to prescribe the future
of the institution most directly concerned. That this failure
is more than an oversight or an expediency is indicated by the
interest shown in developing other separate institutions. For
example, a disfunctional but "proud" military corp, armed with
empty guns, was organized. In addition, there were church, health,
and business subsidiaries, as well as nursery schools, but no
formal education.

One can speculate that the organization did not have sufficient time to develop educational services, but even this specu-
lation presupposes that education or rather "re-education" has
a secondary importance. Such a ranking is inconsistent with
Garvey's aim of revolutionizing the minds of black Americans--
minds which he described as having been consistently misguided.
In terms of this omission, he suffered from a rather mechanistic
view of revolution and nationalism. Because virtually all black
students at that time were attending segregated schools, Garvey
may have mistakenly confounded segregation with separation,
against which DuBois warned. At any rate, he did not recognize
that segregation is closer to cultural integration than to
nationalism.[53]

III. THE UNITY OF HIS TWONESS: CULTURAL NATIONALISM

After the Egyptian and Indian, the Greek and
Roman, the Teuton and Mongolian, the Negro is
a sort of seventh son, born with a veil and gifted
with second-sight in this American world,--a
world which yields him no true self-consciousness,
but only lets him see himself through the reve-
lation of the other world. It is a peculiar sen-
sation, this double-counsciousness, this sense
of always looking at one's self through the eyes
of others, of measuring one's soul by the tape
of a world that looks on in amused contempt and

39

pity. One never feels his two-ness--an American,
a Negro; two souls, two thoughts, two unreconciled
strivings; two warring ideals in one dark body,
whose dogged strength keeps it from being torn
asunder.[54]

The question to be considered is what DuBois meant in the
above statement and what he meant to say at other times on the
same subject.

It is surely the case that black political history is
characterized by this ever present two-ness. It is also likely
that the political consciousness of blacks has been strained, if
not torn asunder, by a two-ness. Yet, consciousness, ideology,
attitudes and the like are phenomenologically distinct from behavior.
The dualism which blacks show on the level of behavior or practice
may reflect an ideological or cultural dualism, but this is only
reflection about identity. There can, and should be, a unity
in "true" self-consciousness.[55] Moreover, DuBois seems to have
attained this self-consciousness of black culture, this conscious
unity of black political culture.

Consciousness of being a black American is by definition a
mixed identity whose parts are in constant tension. American
society has unquestionably projected a very degraded and degrading
image of blacks on blacks, and those who wish to disappear or
melt into that America, must at the same time face their own
worthlessness, a worthlessness reinforced by their attempts to
submerge their identity with the originator of their degradation.
Still, this kind of psychoanalytic interpretation may be going
too far. All such tendencies probably exist, but the assumption
as to primary identity has to be tested for each person.[56] The
premise does not apply to many blacks, including DuBois, who see
themselves not as Black Americans, but as blacks in America. They
may recognize that black culture is interspersed with "Americanisms"
but that cultural identity is nevertheless a single whole.

DuBois expresses this resolved consciousness when he asks
rhetorically:

What after all, am I? Am I an American or am
I a Negro? Can I be both? Or is it my duty to
cease to be a Negro as soon as possible and be
an American?

Is this right? Is it rational? Is it good
policy? Have we in America a distinct mission
as a race--a distinct sphere of action and opportunity for race development, or is self-obliter-

40

ation the highest end to which Negro blood dare
aspire.[57]

This racial blood and its goals are defined by DuBois in
terms of culture which means "more or less vividly conceived
ideals of life."[58] While it does not seem to be his purpose nor
his responsibility to develop an explicit description of black
culture, he did have some ideas. He did, for example, depict
the religiosity he saw as pervasive in black life.[59]

More often, he affirmed the existence of this culture by
calling for its development. In 1920 he said, "let us train
ourselves to see beauty in black," and he added that there is
much to be seen. He saw Pan Africanism as an appropriate expression
of the Black heritage. He indicated that a talented tenth would
cement and reinforce this heritage. Likewise, socialism was seen
as a necessary prevention of the corruptions of black economic
acquisitions.

At the same time, he separates blacks from the "American"
or Anglo-Saxon culture and characterized the latter in harsh but
considered terms. In "Souls of White Folk"[60] he criticizes white
America for its ethnocentricity as well as its "capitalistic"
values. In "White Masters of the World" he attacks the concept
of the gentlemen in all European groups as a pompous defense of
oppression.[61] With this kind of view, black cultural nationalism
is the only real choice.

The distinction between conscious and identificational considerations, on the one hand, and object-oriented dispositions
or attitudes, on the other, is important to our understanding of
ideology. The ideology associated with the black cultural identity
is, as has been indicated, cultural nationalism. In a total concept of ideology its analytic or cognitive component is the individual's definition of himself in his world, and its normative
component is the assertion about the way his world should be. On
the purely political plane blacks are, therefore, identified as
a separate political entity which should pursue its own political
goals. Consequently, with respect to the nationalist-integrationist
question, where nationalism is defined without cultural implications,
DuBois' position is, in some sense, ideologically indeterminate.

Thus the choice on the conscious level for DuBois was between
being or not being black, culturally defined. The choice between
integrationism and nationalism, as generally defined and as exemplified in Section II, is not such a choice. They are perhaps
similar in form but a decision to be black and to promote blackness
does not prescribe a decision on the latter.

41

This thesis has already been evidenced by DuBois' ability to move tactically between integrationist and nationalist policy, while, in his words, "welding them together." Tactical nationalism in terms of a black political party, for example, is only acceptable where goals associated with black cultural development, whether black socialism or Pan Africanism, can be pursued. Similarly, tactical integration is judged acceptable when it accords with the preservation of a black identity. Integration of this sort assumes a cultural pluralism rather than a melting pot society as its context. It does not necessarily suppose blacks can become an ethnic group "just like" European ethnic groups, but it does suppose that there is a sufficient pluralistic base on which to build black ethnic parity with others.[62]

In the framework of cultural nationalism the dissimilarity between nationalistic and integrationistic politics persists, but with diminished importance. It becomes just politics, in the colloquial sense. Tactical nationalism is policy which concerns itself with achieving social goals solely within, and by means of, a solidified black community. Tactical integrationism, on the other hand, is policy which seeks to implement the social goals of a black community and for that community, but within the larger American polity.

There is, therefore, continuity in the dualism of DuBois. A black political party is, in a primary sense, nationalistic because it is concerned with the aggregation and articulation of black interests. However, to the extent that it expects to accommodate those interests to the traditional American electoral system, such a party is integrationist. Likewise, DuBois could reasonably choose to belong to the NAACP with its tradition of integration, while insisting that a black-supported agency would be superior. He also participated in an expressly integrationist socialist party, while calling for a separate socialistically-organized system among blacks. In each case the choice is less a matter of ideology, than of political power accounting.

That the dualism in black politics has not always been viewed in this manner, can be illustrated by the conflicts involving DuBois. The most outstanding case is his rejection of what Cruse calls Washington's economic nationalism. Cruse concludes: "Without ever admitting that Booker T. Washington had indeed been closer to the truth in 1900, DuBois switched his attention to the problem of economic self-sufficiency."[63] However, DuBois did not change his real position but only his emphasis. In 1900 DuBois was concerned with civil rights and higher education as a means of expressing and developing black culture, and thus giving economics a meaningful context. He never returned to Washington's "culturally disembodied" economic program.

In sum, it is useful to find continuity in the DuBois' politics and to explain his disagreement with others by reference to cultural nationalism. Yet, the explanation leads immediately to a related question: Where does DuBois' cultural nationalism fall in the world of black politics? More specifically, what is the meaning of the nationalist-integrationist distinction for those who are outside the DuBois ideology? While he analyzed the politics of those with whom he disagreed, he did not offer a generalized assessment of them. However, a more global classification, encompassing the other forms of politics, can be made in retrospect.

IV. IMPLICATIONS FOR STUDY OF PUBLIC POLICY IN EDUCATION

Broadly applying the term _ideology_ to all aspects of social criticism, we have found in DuBois a powerful critic of black politics, as well as arguments for social and political change. But, we could scarcely expect to find that he fully assessed the place of his ideology in black political history, because he was, at the same time, having a profound effect on the continuing creation of that history. Consequently, the general descriptive hypothesis presented here on that nationalism-integrationism which is not subsumed under cultural nationalism, cannot claim direct support from DuBois' analysis. Still, his discussion of specific events serves as a guide for the analysis of the other nationalism-integrationism, that physically conceived.

It was earlier observed that DuBois was opposed to a policy of school integration which concerned itself with maintaining a statistical balance of black and white faces in the classroom. Rather he sought integration only where educational opportunity was unequal and he remained committed to independent black education, particularly at higher levels. Such independence was an essential part of his cultural nationalism. In contrast, post-"Brown v. the Board of Education" federal policy has given unqualified commitment to school integration.

What is the basis of federal integration policy? It is, in some sense, a recognition, now made into law, that separate has never been equal in American public education. Yet, in another sense, it is judgment of racial difference which defines blacks and whites on the basis of purely physical characteristics.[64] The test of race is a simple visual procedure applied to the individual or his parents. Moreover, if the question of culture is considered, it is relegated to the status of "ivy tower" rhetoric by the demand that such culture fit in, or accommodate itself to, "general American" cultural standards.

43

In part, physical definitions of race may be an unavoidable artifact of legislative drafting because law should be as precise and concrete as possible. However, the possible precision of physical definitions has not been without its awkward consequences and questionable social utility. The major judicial decisions affecting educational integration have sought conceptual precision and simplicity by relying on genetic concepts of race. In consequence, they have lost their potential power for social redirection and their durability as legal precedents largely because the real world shifts among multiple conceptualizations. The Supreme Court opinions in the often cited integration cases of Plessy v. Ferguson and Brown v. Board of Education are pertinent here for their language more than for their policy consequences.

First, introduced as evidence in the Plessy case was the observation that "Plessy, who was of seven-eighths Caucasian and one-eighth African blood" had unlawfully seated himself in a white-only railway coach.[65] In response to this transgression, the Supreme Court ruled:

> The object of the [Fourteenth] Amendment was undoubtedly to enforce the equality of the two races before the law, but in the nature of things it could not have been to abolish distinction based upon color, or to enforce social, as distinguished from political, equality or a commingling of the two races upon terms unsatisfactory to either.[66]

"Distinctions of color" seemed to the Court, and still seem to many in government, such an obvious and primary factor in the race problem that no one stopped to question it. That it is, however, a limited and questionable distinction was hinted when the Warren Court abandoned the more conservative orientation of its predecessors in the 1954 Brown vs. the Board of Education decision. Yet, the Brown decision did not so much abandon the genetic concept of race as it simply muddied or detached the physical from the "interracial" and from "segregation". Thus, the Plessy decision presumed in its reference to "commingling of the two races" that simple contact constitutes the boundary of the critical <u>political distinction</u> on race. The Brown ruling, on the other hand, recognizes a usual relationship between race and psychological factors, e.g. self-consciousness in an interracial environment. Thus it ruled:

> The impact [of segregation] is greater when it has the sanction of the law; for the policy of separating the races is usually interpreted as denoting the inferiority of the Negro group. A

44

sense of inferiority affects the motivation of
a child to learn.[67]

Thus, the Court moves from the simple recognition that members of a racial group have in common a "racial identity" to the
more complex assertion that the nature of that identity is some-
times socio-psychological, or, in other words, that racial identification is not completely described, nor prescribed, by physical
characteristics. The finding that a sense of inferiority attaches
to "being black" in segregated America is a tacit admission that
race, as a social phenomenon, is not simply a result of birth in
as much as "feelings" accompany the racial distinction. Still,
the Court did not make a principled statement about racial identity
but rather concluded that under the particular circumstances there
is a factor which escaped the Court's attention in Plessy vs.
Ferguson.

The findings of the Brown Court, although they have profoundly
affected subsequent legislation and Court decision, have not
significantly transformed conceptualization on social issues.
Accordingly, more recent and presumably more progressive legislation continues on the level of conceptualization found in the
Plessy case. Illustratively, the Massachusetts Racial Imbalance
Law of 1965 observes:

> ...racial imbalance shall be deemed to exist
> when the percent of non-white students in any
> public school is in excess of fifty percent of
> the total number of students in such school.[68]

Notably, the two Court rulings differ in their use of
fractions; while Plessy quantified the individual racial identity,
the Racial Imbalance Law only quantifies the school's racial
identity. Yet, they both (and in some sense Brown too) have in
common the treatment of racial distinctions in purely physical
terms. The Imbalance Law, however, inspired by historical social
scientific insights like those emerging from the Brown ruling,
has given an old concept a new liberal intent.

The Imbalance Law has recently floundered in Massachusetts
partly because liberals have lost interest in supporting it while
conservatives have successfully pursued their attacks on it. The
liberal turn does not automatically signify an ideological slack-
ening, but rather a conceptual reorientation towards the "cultural
consequences of racial integration." Ultimately, such a conceptual reorientation may be tied to ideological change, but
immediately inactivity verging on apathy seems to be the only
consequence. The liberals have failed to outline a new ideological
direction while contenting themselves with staying clear of open

45

conservatism on civil rights. More to the point, they have simply come to recognize, and to feel insecure with, a unidimensional concept in a multi-dimensional world.

In a like manner, nationalism has been "culturally disembodied." To illustrate: the recent black capitalism move, which Cruse identifies with Washington's economic nationalism, does not (vague as it is) seem to concern itself with promoting values that would separate black economics in America. Rather, it seems bent on imposing the ethics of American capitalism on blacks. The same criticism applies to "revolutionary nationalism" if it distinguishes itself by call for liberation, violent or non-violent, without specifying values and goals which grow out of the tradition of black consciousness.

Yet, any specific critique of individual nationalist programs and policies must be more reserved and tentative than a comparable critique of integrationist politics because the task of articulating and promulgating black culture is extraordinarily formidable. For rather obvious historical and sociological reasons it is much simpler to impose black slogans on undefined social phenomena found in the dominant American culture than to attempt to isolate the diverse cultural origins and meanings of these phenomena while maintaining a black nationalist orientation. This problem will be further examined in subsequent chapter.

It seems unreasonable, if not illogical, to conclude that these non-DuBois cases are culturally or ideologically disembodied. The statement can, perhaps, be justified on the grounds that the persons involved have no broader normative commitment, and this is quite feasible. Analytically however, they still fall within a broader framework. The pursuit of integrationist or nationalist policy in America without an explicit commitment to black culture is an implicit concession to that culture which is institutionalized in the United States (Anglo-Saxon, if you will).

We can say these latter kinds of policy are parts of an ideology of "cultural integrationism" as opposed to cultural nationalism. But in the common understanding of ideology, the "ism" is inappropriate because those who are not cultural nationalists do not have to believe in integration of that kind. Still in this case nationalist and integrationist policy that recognizes race as merely physical may have the same consequence as policy resulting from a normative commitment to Anglo-Saxon tradition. While it is too soon to affirm, it should be recognized that black culture can persist and develop in spite of opposing efforts by blacks.

The ideological alternatives discussed in this chapter can be shown to form a mutually exclusive set of categories, as in

46

the following table.

Conceptual Orientation	Normative Orientation ⟶	
↓	Integrationism	Nationalism
Physical	P I	P N
Cultural	C I	C N

   Their exclusivity resides in the totality and/or central
focus of the ideology and not in any single component. As previously
indicated, the two major cognitive and the two normative positions
often lead to overlapping policies and practices. In addition,
those who fall into the fourth quadrant, as does DuBois, are
capable, from time to time, of conforming to a policy coming from
any of the other three quadrants. The others are much less flexible.

   This suggestion should not be taken as an attempt to castigate
nationalism or integrationism which does not fit into DuBois's
framework, but to consider the continuing vitality of DuBois's
thought. He recognized in the black self-consciousness a strong
American element; he recognized a two-ness of mind, but drew a
unified identity out of it. With this perspective he was able to
move flexibly between tactics of integrationism and nationalism;
whereas physically-defined black policies are stuck in a nationalist-integrationist dualism that is irreconcilable. With this kind
of analysis of race, nationalism permits of no association with
whites, to the extent that it is nationalistic, because its identity
depends on physical separation. By the same token, such integration
requires unrelenting physical balance because there is no other
criterion by which to evaluate race relations. DuBois, instead,
saw "souls" separating blacks and whites and decided that the souls
of black folk had in comparison at least as much to recommend
them.

47

CHAPTER II
FOOTNOTES

[1]W.E.B. DuBois, Darkwater: Voices from Within the Veil, (New York: Schocken Books, 1969).

[2]Ibid. "The Souls of White Folks." Also DuBois, The Souls of Black Folk (Greenwich: Fawcett Publications, 1961).

[3]Philip E. Converse, "The Nature of Belief Systems in Mass Publics." ed, David Apter, Ideology and Discontent (New York: The Free Press, 1964), p. 219. The inclusion of terms such as radicalism or extremism would not make a significant difference here.

[4]Ibid., pp. 234-235.

[5]See Theodore Lowi, The End of Liberalism (New York: W.W. Norton & Co., 1969). Lowi argues that "interest group liberalism" is the primary focus of American ideological commitments.

[6]Souls of Black Folk, p. 21.

[7]On the importance of a cultural philosophy see Harold Cruse, The Crisis of the Negro Intellectual (New York: William Morrow & Co. 1967).

[8]See Samuel Bowles, "Unequal Education and the Social Division of Labor," ed. Martin Carnoy, Schooling in a Corporate Society. (New York: David McKay Publishers, 1972), pp. 36-64.

[9]Harold Cruse, The Crisis of the Negro Intellectual. (New York: W. Morrows Co., 1967) p. 226.

[10]Martin Delany, The Condition, Elevation, Emigration, and Destiny of the Colored People of the United States Politically Considered. (Philadelphia, 1852).

[11]See Frederick Douglass, Life and Times of Frederick Douglass New York: Crowell-Collier, 1892) pp. 76-80.

[12]See Martin Delany, "The Political Destiny of the Colored Race," ed. Sterling Stuckey, The Ideological Origins of Black Nationalism (Boston: Beacon Press, 1972) pp. 195-236.

[13]Ibid. p. 203.

[14]Ibid. "Introduction," p. 11.

[15] Francis L. Broderick and August Meier, <u>Negro Protest Thought in the Twentieth Century</u> (Indianapolis: Bobbs-Merrill Co., Inc. 1965) p.6.

[16] Booker T. Washington, <u>Up From Slavery</u> (New York: Doubleday & Co., 1901, 1967) p. 233. He sent an open letter to the Louisiana State Constitutional Convention in 1897.

[17] Broderick and Meier, p. 10.

[18] Washington. Op.cit. p. 155.

[19] Cruse, Op. cit. p. 19 & 21, for example.

[20] Washington, Op. cit. p. 6.

[21] Clifford Geertz, "Ideology As A Cultural System." ed. David Apter, <u>Ideology and Discontent</u>. Op. cit., pp. 58 & 64.

[22] <u>Souls of Black Folk</u>, Op. cit., pp. 43-54.

[23] This is distinguished from his attack on the Tuskegee machine and Washington as a power figure; elaborated in <u>Dusk of Dawn</u>, Op. cit. pp. 71-76.

[24] <u>Souls of Black Folk</u>, Op. cit., p. 45.

[25] Ibid., p. 43.

[26] Ibid., pp. 52-53.

[27] Cruse, op. cit. p. 331.

[28] Broderick and Meier, Op. cit., pp. 40-48. W.E.B. DuBois, "The Talented Tenth." in Booker T. Washington, <u>et al</u>., <u>The Negro Problem</u> (New York: James Pott & Co., 1903).

[29] Marcus Garvey's criticism of DuBois seems ill-founded. See Amy-Jacques Garvey, <u>The Philosophy and Opinions of Marcus Garvey</u>, (New York: Atheneum, 1969), Vol. II, pp. 56-61.

[30] Andrew G. Paschal, "The Spirit of W.E.B. Dubois." <u>The Black Scholar</u> Vol. 2, No.2, October 1970.

[31] DuBois, "The Talented Tenth," Op. cit. p. 41.

[32] Ibid., p. 43.

[33] Ibid., p. 46.

[34]DuBois, The Philadelphia Negro (New York: Schoken Books, 1967) first published 1899.

[35]Paschal, Op.cit., p.21.

[36]Crisis, Vol. 38 (Sept. 1939), p. 314.

[37]Ibid., p. 315.

[38]Paschal, Op.cit., p. 23. From Dubois, "A Negro Nation Within the Nation," Current History, June 1935, p. 270.

[39]See Lorenzo Morris, The Invisible Politics, Chapters 2 and 7, for a more extensive discussion of the consistencies and inconsistencies in approaches to social class and racial-cultural phenomena.

[40]Cruse, Op.cit., p. 564.

[41]Crisis, Vol. 41 (January 1934) "Postscript", p. 20.

[42]Crisis, Vol. 12 (October 1916), p. 268.

[43]Dusk of Dawn, Op. cit., p. 289.

[44]Crisis, Vol. 38 (September 1931), p. 315.

[45]Crisis, Vol. 12 (October 1916), p. 268.

[46]Crisis, Vol. 13 (December 1916), p. 63

[47]Theodore Lowi, The End of Liberalism, (New York: W.W. Norton & Co., 1969).

[48]Broderick, W.E.B. DuBois.... Op. cit., p. 102.

[49]See for example Crisis, Vol. 41 (February 1934) "Postscript."

[50]Crisis, Vol. 40 (September 1933) "On Being Ashamed of Oneself." See also Amy Jacques Garvey, Philosophy and Opinions of Marcus Garvey (New York: Athneum, 1969, (Vol. 11) pp. 39, 56-61.

[51]E. Franklin Frazier in The Negro Church leads to the conclusion there is no such culture, thus there would be nothing upon which Garvey could draw.

[52]Amy Garvey, Op. cit. Vol. II, p. 38.

[53] Garvey's occasional praise of anti-black, white militant groups seems to illustrate his oversight. Although his seriousness at the time is questionable, he found kind words for the Klu Klux Klan, saying that the Klan understood the "destiny" of the races.

[54] DuBois, Souls of Black Folk Op. cit. p. 16-17.

[55] Consider in this regard G.W.F. Hagel, Phenomenology of Mind (New York: Harper & Row, Publishers, 1967).

[56] Hugh F. Butts, M.D. "Black Rage", Freedomways, Vol. 9, No. 1 (Winter 1969) p. 62. Butts makes a similar criticism of Grier and Cobbs influential study Black Rage.

[57] Crisis, Vol. 41 (June 1934) p. 183. Refers to the passage from The Conservation of Races.

[58] DuBois, The Conservation of Races (The American Negro Academy Washington, E.C. Occasional Paper No. 2, 1897).

[59] DuBois, Souls of Black Folk Op. cit. "Of the Faith of the Fathers."

[60] DuBois, Darkwater, Op. cit. "The Souls of White Folk."

[61] DuBois, The World And Africa, Op. cit. pp. 22-23.

[62] This is distinguished from Chuck Stone's "ceteris paribus" thesis which suggests that all things would remain the same. Chuck Stone, Black Political Power in America (New York: Dell Publishing Co., 1968, 1970) p. 43.

[63] Cruse, Op. cit. p. 176.

[64] Physical characteristics refers primarily to biological phenomenon, but socio-economic status and area of residence may, for example, be included here as long as they indicate non-psychological uniformity.

[65] Norman Dorsen, Discrimination and Civil Rights (Boston: Little Brown and Company, 1969) p. 159.

[66] Ibid. See also 163 U.S. 537, 16 S. Ct. 1138. Underlining is my own.

[67] Ibid., p. 169.

[68] Massachusetts General Laws, Ch. 71 (1965) No. 37 D. See also Norman Dorsen, Discrimination and Civil Rights.

CHAPTER III

Ideological Conflict and Misunderstanding in
Federal Decision-Making on School Desegregation

PART I

What is often overlooked in the whole notion of cultural
deprivation is the destructive influence of racism on the dominant
white culture. Its effects have been ignored in the Brown decision, in the Moynihan Report and in countless other governmental
policies and social science research efforts. However, just as the
culture-of-poverty notion contradicts all important positive aspects of the culture concept,[2] so does the idea of cultural
deprivation. In the sense that culture is the entire way of life
followed by a people, it is obvious that each individual is raised
in a culture. As each individual comes to know the world or organize his experience, he comes to share common standards for perceiving, predicting, judging, and acting with other members of
the community.

As it pertains to educational achievement, the cultural
deprivation explanation did not emerge in its present form until
the 1950s and did not receive wide currency and general uncritical
acceptance until after the Brown decision. Although such theories
are often regarded as liberal because they posit environmental
inadequacy rather than genetic inferiority and because they are
often used to support demands for integration; they still suffer
from cultural myopia. Kenneth Clark argues that it is not the
white child per se whose presence leads to higher achievement for
the Negro child who associates with him in class, but the quality
of the education provided because the white child is there that
makes the difference. "To argue, without irrefutable proof, that
this is not the case," says Clark, "is to lend support to a racially
defined environmental theory of academic achievement that is no
less callous in its consequences than a genetic theory of racial
inferiority would be."[3] Yet, racially free environmental theory

of academic achievement presupposes an individual and group self-consciousness that is not dependent on the racial other for its existence. The one-sidedness of the idea of culture in the United States casts doubt over the immediate possibility of achieving such an environment.

In terms of the history of racial consciousness in America, G.W.F. Hegel's discussion of the master and servant relationship is relevant. The servant comes to live by his own work and thus becomes self-reliant and independent, while the master comes to rely on the servant's labor and thus becomes dependent.[4] Thus, despite Clark, one might assume that given equal physical facilities, blacks could achieve "quality education" more readily than whites. However, such an assumption ignores the concept of culture and over-looks three hundred years of black-white relationships.

As it applies to blacks, the master-servant relationship differs basically from that described by Hegel. According to Frantz Fanon:

> For Hegel there is reciprocity; here the master laughs at the consciousness of the slave. What he wants from the slave is not recognition but work. In the same way, the slave here is in no way identifiable with the slave who loses himself in the object and finds in his work the source of his liberation. The Negro wants to be like the master. Therefore he is less independent than the Hegelian slave.
>
> In Hegel the slave turns away from the master and turns toward the object. Here the slave turns toward the master and abandons the object.[5]

For Fanon the slave must "make himself recognized" to attain true self-consciousness. He cannot be granted self-consciousness by his master, rather, he must force it.

In a sense, busing forces recognition. While blacks disagree over its usefulness as an instrument of education, they almost universally believe whites should be made to obey the law of the land. While they once passively watched as their black children were bused past neighborhood schools, they now enjoy the prospect of whites being bused past their neighborhood schools. At last there is reciprocity.

"Governmental Policy and Racial Cognitions"

Those blacks who support the forced busing of white children
are becoming like the master to the extent that he has always
supported the forced busing of black children. Yet support for
the law or governmental policy has another important consequence.
According to Murray Edelman governmental acts are the chief source
of cues as to group status and security, especially as to future
status and security for the great mass of political spectators.
Moreover, "political actions chiefly arouse or satisfy people not
by granting or withholding their stable substantive demands but
rather by changing the demands and the expectations."[6] Thus one
can see that it is not the substantive nature of particular political issue that determines whether a translation into myth[7] will
occur, but rather the mode of cognizing or of apprehending any
issue.

It is in this translating process that the role of culture
becomes crucial. In regard to race relations the dominant historic
myth has been one of white superordinate and black subordinate
status supported by genetic, legal, environmental, and divinely
ordained arguments. The myth helps to stabilize the social order,
especially when reinforced by Jim Crow ordinances and court decisions. In more recent years the myth has come into conflict with
other cognitions, the chief of which has been a norm of divinely
(or popularly) ordained equal rights regardless of race or color,
combined with widely held faith in our progress in achieving that
norm. Both these cognitions have to a great extent, been created
by public policies starting with the Declaration of Independence
and Reconstruction legislation. Since World War II these cognitions
have been dramatically heightened with the desegregation of the
armed forces, the establishment of the Fair Employment Practices
Commission, Supreme Court decisions, the civil rights laws of the
late fifties and sixties, and busing.[8] Busing, however, is unique
among governmental acts in that it marks the end of rising normative expectations and illustrates the differing perceptions of
black and white Americans in regard to racial public policy.

"Historical Perspectives"

Even at its founding the United States represented a contradiction between its normative values—the democratic creed—and
its cognitions in regard to race—as represented in the institution
of slavery. James Madison illustrates the problems such a contradiction raises for governmental policy. In deciding how members of the House of Representatives are to be apportioned,
Madison faces the question of counting slaves as persons or not
at all:

The federal Constitution, therefore, decides with
great propriety on the case of our slaves, when
it views them in the mixed character of persons
and of property. This is in fact their true
character. It is the character bestowed on them
by the laws under which they live; and it will
not be denied, that these are the proper
criterion; because it is only under the pretext
that the laws have transformed the negroes into
subjects of property, that a place is disputed
them in the computation of numbers; and it is
admitted, that if the laws were to restore the
rights which have been taken away, the negroes
could no longer be refused an equal share of
representation with the other inhabitants.[9]

Madison, then underscores the rule of law in shaping cognitions.
Blacks are to be regarded as being of "mixed" character--both
persons and property. However, if laws were to give back the
rights taken from blacks, then blacks are entitled to equal
representation. In other words, the law can make blacks whole
people again, but, as we have seen, it cannot grant self-consciousness. And while the law makers might attempt to reconcile norms and cognitions, they will have little success until
they first achieve racial self-consciousness.

Perhaps it is only fitting that most major court decisions
effecting enforced separation over the past hundred years have
relied on a decision in a Boston case in which a five-year-old girl
was forced to walk past five elementary schools for white children on her way to the public school Boston maintained for Negroes.
In deciding against the plantiff and her attorney, Charles Sumner,
Judge Shaw of the Supreme Judicial Court of Massachusetts stated
that Sumner's invocation of "the great principle" that all persons
ought to stand equal before the law was "perfectly sound" and
"animates the whole spirit of our constitution of free government"
but...

when this great principle comes to be applied
to the actual and various conditions of persons
in society, it will not warrant the assertion,
that men and women are legally clothed with
the same civil and political powers, and that
children and adults are legally to have the
same functions and be subject to the same treatment; but only that the rights of all, as they
are settled and regulated by law, are equally
entitled to the paternal consideration and
protection of the law, for their maintence and

55

security. What these rights are, to which
individuals, in the infinite variety of circumstances by which they are surrounded in
society, are entitled, must depend upon laws
adapted to their respective relations and conditions.[10]

Aside from its prominence as a precedent, the opinion in Roberts vs.
City of Boston in 1849 is notable for three reasons. First, the
judge failed to cite any foundation in reason for the discrimination
practiced by the Boston school committee. Second, he asserted
that school segregation was for the good of both races although
blacks had no part in making the law. Finally, by stating that
the laws are adapted to the respective conditions and relations
of the races, the door is left open for legal change as social
conditions change.

Given that the Civil Rights Act of 1866 and the 13th, 14th,
and 15th Amendments are attempts to reconcile belief and practice,
the Supreme Court reveals its divided thinking in the Slaughter-
house Cases. In dealing with a challenge to the monopoly over the
butchering business granted to a company by the Louisiana legislature in 1869, the Court made a distinction between United States
citizenship and state citizenship. The Court decided that the
federal government could not usurp the states' authority to manage
"those fundamental civil rights for the security and establishment
of which organized society is instituted."[11] Yet the split over
the decision and the vague language of the opinion left in doubt
what exactly those rights were.

In 1896 the Supreme Court took a giant step in defining the
rights of states in <u>Plessy vs. Ferguson</u>; Homer Plessy, who was
only one-eighth Negro and looked white, was arrested when he refused to leave a white compartment on a train. Louisiana law
stipulated that even persons of one-thirty-second Negro extraction
were to be classed as Negroes. Plessy brought suit and in 1896
the Supreme Court rejected his plea that segregation laws violated
the equal protection clause of the Fourteenth Amendment (<u>Plessy v.
Ferguson</u>). Looking at the Court's decision we can see that it
assumes a cognitive orientation of genetic difference but a normative position of racial neutrality. In the words of Justice Henry
B. Brown's majority opinion:

The object of the (Fourteenth) Amendment was
undoubtedly to enforce the absolute equality
of the two races before the law, but in the nature
of things it could not have been intended to
abolish distinctions based upon color, or to

enforce social, as distinguished from political
equality or a commingling of the two races upon
terms unsatisfactory to either. Laws permitting,
and even requiring, their separation in places
where they are liable to be brought into contact
do not necessarily imply the inferiority of
either... We consider the underlying fallacy of
the plaintiff's argument to consist in the assumption that the enforced separation of the two
races stamps the colored race with a badge of
inferiority. If this be so, it is not by reason
of anything found in the act, but solely because
the colored race chooses to put that construction
upon it... Legislation is powerless to eradicate
racial instincts read cognitive orientations
or to abolish distinctions based upon physical
differences, and the attempt to do so can only
result in accentuating the difficulties of the
present situation.[12]

With only Justice John Harlan dissenting, this "separate but
equal" doctrine became the basis for school policy.

     Along with playing fast-and-loose with court precedents leading
to Plessy and ignoring the intent of the Fourteenth Amendment,[13]
Justice Brown's opinion seems to reverse the thinking of the founding
fathers, especially Madison. According to Brown, laws cannot affect
how men think about and react to racial differences and there can
be no harm in laws that are based upon and emphasize those differences. In other words, the circle is complete. What law initially
sanctioned as the proper treatment of those with "mixed" character
is reversed. Even though the social and political conditions have
changed, the law is now based on what has become the custom.

     In regard to black cognitions, Judge Brown asserts that any
feelings of inferiority due to state-enforced separation are merely
in the eyes of the beholder. However, like Judge Shaw in the
Roberts case, he fails to cite any logical justification for such
separation. Even custom in Louisiana had permitted integrated
railroad cars for some years after the Civil War. Even Justice
John Harlan, who vigorously dissented from the majority opinion
in Plessy citing the "color-blind" character of the Constitution,
was inconsistent on racial issues. Writing the Court's opinion
in Cumming v. Richmond County Board of Education in 1899 he states:

     While all admit that the benefits and burdens
     of public taxation must be shared by citizens
     without discrimination against any class on
     account of their race, the education of people

in schools maintained by state taxation is a
matter belonging to the respective states, and
any interference on the part of Federal authority
with the management of such schools cannot be
justified except in the case of a clear and
unmistakable disregard of rights secured by
the supreme law of the land. We have here no
such case to be determined.[14]

Once again it was unclear just what rights were secured for blacks
by the Constitution.

It was not until 1954 that the Supreme Court decided they
did have a determination to make in regard to "separate but equal"
schools. Three aspects of the Court's ruling in Brown v. Topeka
Board of Education are of particular interest to our discussion:
1) the use of psychological data to support the decision; 2) the
political nature of the decision; and 3) the implementation of the
decision.

In Plessy, Judge Brown referred to the imputation of inferiority being solely in the mind of the Negro. Kenneth Clark and
his social science colleagues in Brown took that argument to its
logical conclusion and stated that such feelings of inferiority
resulting from state-action were a denial of "equal protection"
under the Fourteenth Amendment. Clark and his wife Mamie cited
as evidence of the psychological damage caused by racial separation the results of several tests they had conducted. In a doll
test to measure children's awareness of their negritude the majority
of Negro children tested indicated an unmistakable preference for
the white doll and a rejection of the brown doll. In a coloring
test, 52 percent of the children preferred to color members of the
opposite sex white or an irrelevant color. This "awareness" of
color was present even in three-year-olds.[15]

Professor Clark's initial testimony in Briggs was subject
to only a superficial cross-examination. Yet latter-day commen-
tators have shown that the test results were open to challenge.
The sample size in Briggs was small and the questions were leading.
Moreover the answers seemed predetermined in that if black children said a brown doll is like themselves, Clark inferred that
segregation had made them conscious of race; while if they said a
white doll was like themselves, he inferred that segregation had
forced them to evade reality.[16] Even Clark was troubled by the
finding that segregated Southern children were less pronounced in
their preference for the white doll than unsegregated Northern
children. Reporting on the crayon test in his 1955 book Prejudice
and Your Child Clark states that "Nearly 80 percent of the Southern
children colored their preferences brown, whereas 36 percent of the

Northern children did." [17] One can assume from these results that self-consciousness was damaged less with segregation and more with integration or one can assume--as did Clark--that the black children of the South were more adjusted to the feeling that they were not as good as whites and accepting defeat at an early age, did not bother to use the device of denial. For Clark this was not true self-consciousness but rather adjustment to a pathology: "Prejudice is something inside people. Segregation is the objective expression of what these people have inside." [18]

While Clark's work was mentioned first in a footnote of the Brown decision, the Justices seemed more concerned with a reference to Gunnar Myrdals An American Dilemma in the same footnote. Both Justice Tom Clark and Hugo Black thought the reference would offend the South. Their objections illustrate the political nature of the decision. The Supreme Court had postponed oral arguments on Brown and Briggs and noted jurisdiction over Davis until at least a month after the 1954 Presidential elections. In consolidating the cases into Brown, Justice Clark noted that "the whole question would not smack of being a purely Southern one." [19]

While the Justices were concerned with Plessy as a precedent, Justice Jackson had previously written that "the judge who can take refuge in a precedent does not need to justify his decision to the reason." [20] Modern conditions may come into conflict with historical doctrine. In other words, a new consciousness may be dominant. Clearly the Justices could find no reasonable excuse for segregated schools. Justice Burton asked the plaintiff's chief counsel, John Davis, if the relations between the two races had changed enough since the adoption of the Fourteenth Amendment to make what might have been unconstitutional then constitutional now. Davis replied "that changed conditions may affect policy, but changed conditions cannot broaden the terminology of the Constitution. The thought is an administrative or a political one, and not a judicial one." [21] Davis added that circumstances--like the development of interstate commerce--might bring new facts within the purview of the constitutional provision, but that they did not affect the language the framers of the Constitution had employed. Justice Felix Frankfarter asked Davis if "equal" were a less fluid term than "commerce between the states," that is did history put a gloss on "equal" which did not permit elimination at admixture of white and colored; to which the southern attorney replied "yes, I am saying that." [22] (Note that the Court upheld the Constitutionality of the 1964 Civil Rights Act by referring to federal control over interstate commerce in Heart of Atlanta Motel v. U.S. and Katzenbach v. McClung.)

Justice Jackson took a different approach in stating that the only valid reason to warrant the Court's decision was "not a change

in the Constitution but in the Negro population."[23] According to
Jackson the Negroes of today were "a different people" from those
"lately freed from bondage" and that societal assimilation was making
inroads that segregation could not stop. While it was clear to
most of the Justices that the Court had steadily been moving in the
direction of declaring segregation based on race unconstitutional
since Gainn v. United States in 1915 and while there was no logical
reason to impose segregation if the white majority did not believe
blacks to be inferior, the question remained of how to implement
the decision.

The NAACP had believed segregation itself was the evil--and
not a symptom of the deeper evil of racism. They attached no importance to the ratio of blacks to whites in South Carolina schools.[24]
Yet it was not reasonable to expect the court to order several
hundred white children in the Clarendon district to be mixed indis-
criminately with the black children who outnumbered them nine to
one. Moreover it was not clear how the United States government
under the command of Republicans in both the Executive and Legislative branches would react. Unfortunately, the implementation
decree--rendered in Brown II--pandered to the Southern temperment
with its "all deliberate speed" order. Kenneth Clark and other
social psychologists warned that delay would breed resistance.
In the absence of Presidential and Congressional support Brown was
virtually ignored by Southern school districts.

While Plessy had assumed that the alternative to segregation
was the "enforced commingling" of the races, Brown had assumed that
a change in the law would be met with good faith compliance.
Segregation had limited individual freedom while Brown sought to
enlarge it. Yet the implementation of that freedom ignored the
history of black-white relations in this country. The government
could not simply step aside and view race neutrally after shaping
the cognitions of both races for almost two hundred years.

CHAPTER III
FOOTNOTES
Part I

[1]Part I and Part II is a loose analogy to the two parts of the
Brown decision--the finding and the implementation. "Twenty-
five miles apart" refers to the decision of Dentucky's Supreme
Court in Berea College v. Kentucky which upheld the state laws
separation of the races in educational institutions but declared
the provision that a biracial school teaching members of both
races at the same time must do it separately in classes at least
twenty-five miles apart a bit arbitrary.

[2]Charles A. Valentine, Culture and Poverty (Chicago: University
of Chicago Press, 1968) p. 15.

[3]Kenneth Clark, Pathos of Power (N.Y.: Harper and Row, 1974) p. 108.

[4]See G.W.F. Hegel, The Phenomenology of the Mind (N.Y.: Harper &
Row, 1967 Baillie translation) pp. 234-239.

[5]Frantz Fanon, Black Skin, White Masks (N.Y.: Grove Press, 1967)
pp. 220-221 (footnote). Fanon's discussion of the Negro may
be compared to the distinction O. Mannoni makes in Prospero and
Caliban between inferiority complexes and dependence. Mannoni
states that inferiority complexes are very exceptional in fairly
homogeneous communities like the Malagasies where the social
framework is still fairly strong. Only those Malagasies who
are thoroughly Europeanized appear suceptable. Dependence involves a totally different mentality and is not compatible with
inferiority (p. 40). What seems to emerge from this comparison
is that color, or more precisely culture, has a mediating effect.
Those with the same culture are dependent upon one another for
recognition. However, those of different culture trying to
adopt the attributes of the master can develop feelings of inferiority.

[6]Murray Edelman, Politics as Symbolic Action (Chicago: Markham,
1971) p. 7.

[7]Edelman defines myth as a belief held in common by a large group
of people that gives events and actions a particular meaning;
it is typically socially used rather than empirically based.
Self-conceptions are created through acceptance of a general
belief, or myth about the course of events. (Edelman, p. 14).

[8]Ibid., p. 18.

[9] James Madison, "Federalist No. 54" in Saul K. Padover (ed.) The Forging of American Federalism, Selected Writings of James Madison (N.Y.: 1965) p. 214.

[10] Richard Kluger, Simple Justice (N.Y.: Knopf, 1976) p. 76.

[11] Ibid., p. 58.

[12] Thomas Dye, The Politics of Equality (Indianapolis: Bobbs-Merrill, 1971) p. 15.

[13] See Kluger's discussion of the Plessy decision in Simple Justice, pp. 78-82.

[14] Kluger, Simple Justice, p. 83.

[15] Ibid., pp. 317-318.

[16] See Edmond Cahn in Kluger, Simple Justice, p. 355.

[17] Kenneth Clark quoted in Kluger Simple Justice, p. 356.

[18] Kenneth Clark quoted in Kluger Simple Justice, p. 495.

[19] Kenneth Clark quoted in Kluger Simple Justice, p. 540. A case from the State of Delaware, Gefhart v. Belton was also consolidated into Brown giving it more geographic diversity. In addition, Bolling v. Sharpe, a suit to desegregate the District of Columbia's schools was heard as a companion case. It is interesting to note that in Bolling the U.S. District Court cited Plessy to justifly segregated schools in the District of Columbia. In 1896, in Plessy, the Supreme Court had cited congressional approval of separate schools in the District of Columbia as one legitimizing reason to uphold segregation. Thus the courts had once again come full circle in justifying segregation. (Kluger, pp. 522-523).

[20] Justice Jackson in Kluger, Simple Justice, p. 604.

[21] John Davis in Kluger, Simple Justice, p. 573.

[22] Richard Kluger, Simple Justice, p. 573.

[23] Justice Jackson in Kluger, Simple Justice, p. 690.

[24] Robert Carter in Kluger, Simple Justice, p. 534.

CHAPTER III

PART II

Can the terms liberal and conservative be used to describe
racial public policy in America? Is busing a conservative or
liberal issue? If it is liberal why is it opposed by northern
Democrats like Representative James O'Hara of Michigan and
Senator Joseph Biden of Delaware and groups like the National
Black Assembly? If it is conservative why is it supported by
the NAACP and Senators Javits and Mondale? Moreover, are institutions like Congress, the Supreme Court, and the Executive
branch inherently liberal or conservative on matters of race?
Certainly the act of busing in itself is nothing new in American
education. Even today approximately the same percentage of education funds are spent on school transportation now as were spent
forty years ago (3.6% v. 3.5%). Yet people's perceptions of
the purpose behind busing have changed along with governmental
support for those purposes.

Strangely enough during the Twentieth Century the Supreme
Court (America's least democratic institution) has been perceived
by blacks as the most favorable respondent to black demands.[1]
Certainly the role of the Supreme Court in national policy-making
is beyond question. However, the influence and independence of
the Court relative to other political institutions remains a subject of debate. Wallace Mendelson has argued that "court intru-
sion upon national policy has thrived in the United States only
in periods of unusual weakness in our party system."[2] According
to Robert Dahl the Court's decisions are generally supportive of
the policies emerging from other political institutions although
a time lag is often involved.[3] A recent article by Jonathan
Casper challenges Dahl's interpretation of his own evidence and
his exclusion of the activities of the Court in statutory construction and in cases arising out of states and localities.
The Warren Court in particular played a leading role in giving
legitimacy to the claims of black citizens and "was crucial to
the development of organizations and activities that eventually
succeeded not only in the streets but in Congress as well."[4]
Thus it would appear that the Supreme Court's policy-making role
might be more important for its symbolic nature in cueing people's
perceptions (cognitive) than its substantive aspect which may be
subject to indifference or evasion (normative).

It was not until after the civil rights demonstrations of
the early sixties that the Congress and Executive Branch moved
to support school desegregation. First, the exposure of the brutal
treatment of civil rights demonstrators at the hands of local

63

officials throughout the South provided public support for federal
action. Second, passage of the Civil Rights Act in 1964 gave the
executive branch power to end discrimination. Under Title IV
of the Civil Rights Act, the Department of Justice could bring
suits against school districts maintaining segregation. Under
Title VI, federal funds could be cut-off to any program in a district that practices segregation. Yet while these titles provide
Justice and HEW officials with the tools to promote integration
they also defined desegregation in a manner excluding racial
balance.

Both Title IV and Title VI of the Civil Rights Act of 1964
contained statutory limitations on the busing of students to correct
racial balance. Under Title IV, section 401 (b) of that Act,
desegregation is defined to mean:

> ...the assignment of students to public schools
> and within such schools without regard to their
> race, color, religion or national origin, but
> 'desegregation' shall not mean the assignment
> of students to public schools in order to over-
> come racial imbalance.[5]

Some members of Congress were still unconvinced that this
definition of desegregation would preclude the efforts of federal
officials to balance schools racially. As a result, two more
provisions were added to Title IV to make clear the position of
the Congress on racial balance schemes. Section 407, the section
empowering the Attorney General to bring desegregation suits,
was made to read "that nothing herein shall empower any official
or court of the United States to issue any order seeking to
achieve a racial balance in any school by requiring the transportation of pupils or students from one school to another or
one school district to another in order to achieve such racial
balance . . . ." In addition Congress added, in section 410
that "nothing in this title shall prohibit classification and
assignment for reasons other than race, color, religion, or national
origin."

Senator Hubert Humphrey, floor manager of the 1964 Civil
Rights Bill, stated that these additional provisions applied to
the entire bill, and especially to any refusal or termination
of federal assistance under Title VI. Senator Humphrey said:

> This addition seeks simply to preclude an
> inference that the title confers new authority
> to deal with 'racial imbalance' in schools, and
> should serve to soothe fears that Title IV
> might be read to empower the Federal Government

to order the busing of children around a city
in order to achieve a certain racial balance
or mix in schools. . . . Furthermore, a new
section 410 would explicitly declare that 'nothing in this title shall prohibit classification
and assignment for reasons other than race,
color, religion, or national origin' . . . .

Thus, classification along bona fide neighborhood school lines, or for any other legitimate reason which local school boards might see
fit to adopt, would not be affected by Title IV,
so long as such classification was bona fide.
Furthermore, this amendment makes clear that
the only Federal intervention in local schools
will be for the purpose of preventing denial of
equal protection of the laws.[6]

It should be noted that the prohibition applies only to transportation across school lines to achieve racial balance. The
transporting of students as part of a freedom of choice plan is
not prohibited. We should also point out that the Act did not
grant any new judicial authority. However, Humphrey did refer
to the impact of court decisions in writing the legislation.

In response to Senator Byrd's (West Virginia) request that
Humphrey give assurance "that under Title VI school children
may not be bussed from one end of the community at taxpayers'
expense to relieve so-called racial imbalance in the schools,"
the floor manager replied:

I do . . . . That language is to be found
in Title IV. The provision [section 407 (a)
(2)] merely quotes the substance of a recent
court decision which I have with me, and which
I desire to include in the Record today, the
so-called Gary case.

Senator Humphrey continued:

Judge Beamer's opinion in the Gary case is
significant in this connection. In discussing
this case, as we did many times, it was decided
to write the thrust of the court's opinion into
the proposed substitute.[7]

In essence the Gary case (Bell) established the validity
of school districts in which de facto segregation existed. If

65

school districts were drawn on the basis of such factors as density of population, travel distances, safety of the children, cost of operating the school system, and convenience to parents and children, and not on the basis of race, then those districts were valid even if there were a racial imbalance caused by discriminatory practices in housing. Senator Humphrey concluded his explanation of the legislation as follows: "The bill does not attempt to integrate the schools, but it does attempt to eliminate segregation in the schools."

This explanation of the purpose of the legislation may appear confusing to those who regard integration and segregation in purely physical terms--an either-or situation. Government has always defined race and race relations in such physical terms, while it was often meant to express a cultural phenomenon.[8] In examining the legislative history of the provisions discussed, it is clear that they were intended to preclude actions by federal officials to correct de facto (chance) segregation as distinguished from de jure (enforced) segregation. Congressman William Cramer, the author of the amendment that defined desegregation in such a manner as to exclude balancing activities, said: "De facto segregation is racial imbalance."[9]

The key to understanding the distinctions made by Humphrey and Cramer lies in the cultural aspect of their explanations. Government attempts to integrate community schools would not reflect the cognitive orientations of those represented by the Minnesota Senator and the Florida Congressman. Yet the elimination of segregation, de jure style, squares with the cultural values of most of their constituents. Most whites have viewed integration from a cultural perspective because their physical appearance was not an obstacle. Hence, de facto segregation, in one sense, is a state of integration. This position has led to disputes over racial balancing plans to overcome de facto segregation. Many blacks, by contrast, have viewed integration from a physical perspective because their physical appearance has always presented a problem, whether buying a home or entering a school or restaurant. Thus, for blacks, integration would imply the elimination of both de jure and de facto segregation. Racial imbalance cannot be separated into the categories of chance and enforced because black cognitive orientations and cultural values are fused (or at least not in acute disjunction).

The busing issue next resurfaced in 1966, during consideration of amendments to the Elementary and Secondary Education Act of 1965. Congressman James O'Hara of Michigan introduced two amendments concerning the use of federal school aid to overcome racially imbalanced schools. O'Hara's first amendment warned federal officials against using the authority granted to them in

66

the 1965 Act to "require the assignment or transportation of students
or teachers in order to overcome racial imbalance." In his second
amendment the Michigan Congressman asked for the deletion of
"racially imbalanced" and "any other condition that has imposed
a substantial and continuing financial burden upon" a school agency
from among the conditions to which the Commissioner of Education
was required to give special consideration in making grants under
Title III of the Elementary and Secondary Education Act of 1965.
This title provides grants to strengthen state departments of
education.

In the debate on the amendments Congressman O'Hara refers
to Title VI of the Civil Rights Act of 1964:

> In the first place, title VI of the Civil
> Rights Act deals with segregation and it in no
> way deals with any so-called racial imbalance.
> It deals with racial discrimination and racial
> segregation. It gives no warrant or authority
> to deal with so-called racial imbalance. And
> nothing in this act ESEA would permit requir-
> ing correction of racial imbalance, absent racial
> discrimination or segregation prohibited by
> title VI of the Civil Rights Act of 1964.[10]

Congressman Powell of New York supported the amendment barring
federal involvement in assignment or transportation; however,
his colleague from New York, Mr. Goodell requested clarification
of the distinction between racial imbalance and discrimination.

> Mr. GOODELL. Title VI (1964 Civil Rights Act)
> I think, and it is the gentleman's assumption
> and mine, bars discrimination?
>
> Mr. O'HARA of Michigan. That is correct.
>
> Mr. GOODELL. But it does not bar defacto racial
> imbalance as such.
>
> Mr. O'HARA of Michigan. It does not bar defacto
> racial imbalance when and if it results without
> any intention to discriminate on the basis of
> race--when it is not the result of discrimi-
> nation.[11]

The second amendment deleted the term "racially imbalanced" from
Subsection (c) in order to make that Subsection consistent with
their first amendment. Both amendments were agreed to.

It is interesting to note that in the foregoing discussion
the phrase de facto segregation was replaced by the phrase de
facto racial imbalance. De jure segregation was referred to
as discrimination.

In 1967, the busing issue was discussed at some length by
Congress on at least three occasions. Each of these discussions
referred to the language of the 1964 Civil Rights Act. The busing
issue first surfaced in connection with the HEW appropriation bill
for fiscal 1968. In its report on the bill, the Senate Appropriations Committee recommended that none of the funds provided
for the Office of Education "be used for busing of public school
students or for any other activities calculated to eliminate racial
imbalance in the public schools." When the measure came to the
floor of the Senate, Senator Javits revealed that Senator Byrd
of West Virginia had urged this prohibition. Senator Byrd responded by saying that the language was inserted "to put the Office
of Education on notice that the committee does not expect to see
any funds in this bill used to bus students in America with the
calculated intent of doing so to eliminate racial imbalance."

The West Virginia Senator believed that such busing was not
mandated by either the 1964 Civil Rights Act or by the Supreme
Court. According to Byrd, forced busing

> . . . flies squarely in the face of the 1964
> Civil Rights Act, in which the word "desegregation"
> was stated not to mean the assignment of students
> to public schools in order to overcome racial
> imbalance. Moreover, forced integration of
> public school children has never been required
> by any U.S. Supreme Court decisions nor has
> there been any decision of that Court requiring
> the elimination of racial imbalance in the public
> schools.13

However, Byrd did not object to busing for other purposes, such
as relieving overcrowded conditions.

The busing issue emerged again three months later during
the consideration of the District of Columbia appropriations
bill for fiscal 1968. On this occasion the Senate Appropriations
Committee added a section to the bill prohibiting use of funds
for the "assignment or transportation of students to public
schools in the District of Columbia in order to overcome racial
imbalance." Judging from the ensuing debate, it seems clear that
the prohibition was motivated, at least in part, by Judge Skelly
Wright's order in Hobson v. Hansen. This case was viewed by
the court as a "test [of] the current compliance of [the D.C.]

schools with the principles announced in Bolling v. Sharpe, its
companion case, Brown v. Board of Education of Topeka, and their
progeny." Finding discrimination in the public schools of the
"capital of the greatest country on earth," Judge Wright ordered
various steps to eliminate it, including "transportation for
volunteering children in overcrowded school districts east of
Rock Creek Park to underpopulated schools west of the Park."14

Senators Javits of New York and Byrd of West Virginia were
once again at the center of the debate. Senator Byrd contended
that there were underpopulated schools on both sides of Rock
Creek Park and that the busing of students in this case was both
unnecessary and illegal. Senator Javits countered that, in effect,
the West Virginia Senator was expressing a personal opinion.
Byrd agreed but also stated that the legislative history of busing
was clear on the point of busing to overcome racial imbalance.
He specifically referred to his June 4, 1964 exchange with
Senator Humphrey on Title IV of the 1964 Civil Rights Act. Byrd
also added that "the U.S. Supreme Court has never ruled against
racial imbalance in the schools as long as that imbalance is
not the result of State action of a discriminatory nature."15

A month later the busing issue was to come up again during
Senate consideration of the Elementary and Secondary Education
Act of 1967. Senator Dirksen of Illinois offered the following
anti-busing amendment:

> No funds authorized in this or any other
> Act shall be used to pay any costs of the
> assignment or transportation of students or
> teachers in order to overcome racial imbalance.16

Senator Dirksen, who had played a leading role in passage of the
1964 Act, said that his amendment would carry out the intent of
section 407 of that Act. Hinting that some federal officials
were deliberately violating the law, the Illinois Senator said
that "[i]n section 407 . . . we made it plain . . . that no official of the United States or court of the United States is em-
powered to issue any order seeking to achieve racial balance in
any school by requiring the transportation of pupils or students
from one school to another, in order to achieve such racial
balance." 17 Dirksen went on to refer to the oft-quoted exchange
between Senators Humphrey and Robert Byrd on Title IV of the
1964 Civil Rights Act.

Senator Hruska of Nebraska joined the debate by stating that
he believed Judge Wright's action in Hobson v. Hansen violated
both Title IV of the 1964 Act and Title VI of the Elementary and

Secondary Education Act of 1965. Senator Dirksen agreed adding
"[n/ ow, either we compel the agencies of Government to treat
these things we do with respect, or otherwise apply the kind of
discipline that our form of government still makes available."[18]
Dirksen went on to say that the legislative branch of the
Government can abolish any agency or any court "including Judge
Skelly Wright and his job, if he so desires."[19]

Senators Morse of Oregon and Griffin of Michigan led the
fight against the Dirksen amendment. Griffin pointed out a
crucial difference between the Dirksen amendment and Title IV
of the 1964 Civil Rights Act. Griffin argued the following:

> . . . the Dirksen amendment is not a restatement
> of the language in title IV of the Civil Rights
> Act. It goes further. It prohibits the use of
> Federal funds in an instance where there is no
> requirement but it is purely a matter of local
> policy. [20]

Senator Morse, floor manager of the bill, stated that he would not
support any action by the Federal Government which directed or
dictated to the States what their educational policy should be,
"unless I can be shown in a specific case that a constitutional
issue is involved and a State seeks to do something that is
unconstitutional."[21]

Griffin offered an amendment to the Dirksen amendment that
would leave the matter of busing in the hands of local officials.
Griffin's amendment was defeated in a tie vote and Senator Kennedy
of New York moved to reconsider the vote. Dirksen moved to defeat
the Kennedy motion by a tabling motion. The Dirksen tabling motion
was rejected and the Senate then adopted the Kennedy motion. However, the next day Senator Dirksen withdrew his amendment—
thus killing the Griffin amendment—before it ever came to a vote.

By this time the pattern of annual anti-busing amendments to
HEW appropriations bills or efforts directed to that end had
become fairly well set. Thus, when the House Appropriations
Committee reported that agency's appropriations measure for fiscal
1969 with a pair of provisions intended to curb federal encourage-
ment of or involvement in busing schemes, it came as no surprise.
These two provisions (sections 409 and 410) read as follows:

> (Sec. 409) No part of the funds contained in
> this Act may be used to force busing of students,
> abolishment of any school, or to force any student
> attending any secondary school to attend a partic-
> ular school against the choice of his or her parents

70

or parent.
(Sec. 410) No part of the funds contained in
this Act shall be used to force busing of students,
the abolishment of any school or the attendance
of students of a particular school as a condition
precedent to obtaining Federal funds otherwise
available to any State, school district, or
school.[22]

Congressman Cohelan of California offered two amendments to
delete sections 409 and 410 from the bill. He argued that these
sections prohibited the use of federal incentives to require
affirmative action to integrate the schools. Mr. Whitten responded, in part, as follows:

Our Appropriations Committee for the past 2 or
3 years has written in its report that the Department of Education has been going beyond the law
in this area and has called on it to cease. The
Department has refused, or rather ignored these
directives, leaving our only recourse to write
these provisions into law.[23]

Mr. Whitten went on to say the following:

The Civil Rights Act, as far as integration,
says what can and cannot be done and says what
integration requires. HEW simply does not have
the right to direct anyone to do either of these
things . . . . It just withholds the funds
until it gets people to do these things.[24]

Congressman Joelson of New Jersey asked if the schools having
their funds withheld were integrated. The Mississippi Congressman replied that they were "but they do not force people to go
where they do not want to, except where such course has been
necessary to satisfy HEW or to satisfy a court order."[25]

This latter statement seemed to get at the heart of the
debate. In the previous month the Supreme Court had issued a
decision in <u>Green</u> <u>v.</u> <u>New</u> <u>Kent</u> <u>County, Va.</u> which declared that
the "freedom-of-choice" plan in itself was not an end if it failed
to undo segregation. Thus, Congressman Goodell argued that
Mr. Whitten's view of integrated schools raised a question of
definition. Obviously the Supreme Court did not believe that
merely to open up all the schools in a community constituted
integration. In supporting the amendments, Congressman Cellar
of New York quoted Roy Wilkins in regard to the Whitten proposal:

71

$\lfloor$it$\rfloor$ would restrict efforts to eliminate the
badly discredited 'freedom of choice' plans,
plans which by seeming to allow students to choose
their own schools, often in atmospheres heavy with
intimidation, have resulted in virtually no desegregation at all.[26]

Mr. Cohelan reported that more than two million Negro students
were still segregated in eleven States despite the thunderous
protests of the South.

Mr. Whitten continued to maintain that "$\lfloor$t$\rfloor$here is not a
single Negro in the South that is not free to go to any school
he wants to . . ." and therefore the schools were integrated.
Mr. Thompson of Georgia expressed concern that the amendment
was being referred to as an anti-South amendment. Yet he
believed it might be considered "an anti-North amendment when it
comes to the busing of students."[27]

It was at this point that Congressman Quie of Minnesota
stated the crux of the debate:

> Last year we amended section 704 of the ESEA to
> make certain that the U.S. Office of Education
> could not use any funds to 'require the assign-
> ment of transportation of students or teachers
> in order to overcome racial imbalance.' I supported
> that amendment. Now the Whitten amendment goes
> too far. It would prevent the local school dis-
> trict from busing students, closing a school or
> assigning a student to a school without a parent's
> approval using title I ESEA money. This would
> be true even if the local school district felt
> it was a wise use of the title I money to help
> disadvantaged children. This is federal control
> of education which I do not support.[28]

While Northern congressmen would and did support measures to
prohibit the forced busing of children to overcome racial
imbalance, they would not expand the prohibition to the aboli-
tion of schools or freedom-of-choice plans.

The House rejected the Cohelan amendments but the Senate
saved the bill for Northern liberals. The Senate Appropriations
Committee added the following crucial prepositional phrase to
each section of the Whitten provisions: "in order to overcome
racial imbalance." This measure was eventually passed by the
Senate and sent to conference with the committee recommended
langauge in sections 409 and 410.

72

In the debate on the conference report Mr. Cohelan again
stated the question before the House:

> The question is whether the Federal Govern-
> ment should be able to effectively encourage
> desegregation in schools which are unconstitution-
> ally segregated.

> The question has nothing to do with forced
> busing of students.

> It has nothing to do with correction of de
> facto segregation. In fact the Senate language
> which I support over the conference language
> specifically provides that funds may not be
> withheld for failure to deal with racial imbal-
> ance.[29]

Despite objections in both the House and Senate the conference report was adopted. It was now becoming clear to those
Representatives and Senators from the South that it would be
difficult to get Northern support prohibiting busing and other
controversial desegregation plans that did not involve "racial
imbalance" (de facto segregation). The appeals of Senators Stennis
and Byrd to the Humphrey-Byrd exchange on the 1964 Civil Rights
Act were not seen as relevant to the conference report.

Less than a year later the House and Senate would engage
in a debate strikingly similar to the 1968 consideration of the
Whitten amendments. Once again the House Appropriations
Committee reported a HEW 1970 fiscal appropriations bill containing
the identical Whitten provisions it had reported in 1968. Sections
408 and 409, like their predecessors, stipulated that no funds
in the bill could be used to "force" busing, school relocation or
student assignments against the wishes of any parent or as a
condition for obtaining federal funds.

Congressman Cohelan of California offered two amendments to
strike sections 408 and 409 from the bill. He stated that the
Whitten provisions jeopardized the progress made since the enactment of civil rights legislation:

> During the 1967-68 school year--mark this--
> 13.9 percent of Negro students in the South
> attended racially integrated schools. Last
> year this figure increased to 30.3 percent. Under
> the present law we can expect an increase to about
> 40 percent this coming year.[30]

73

The California Congressman believed that if sections 408 and 409 remained, we could expect retrenchment to 10 or 5 percent. He also cited the Green decision (rejecting freedom-of-choice plans) as a key to desegregation efforts.

Mr. Casey, chairman of the subcommittee handling the HEW appropriation, argued that that agency had exceeded its authority in destroying local control. Mr. Cohelan asked, "[h]ow else do you enforce title VI of the Civil Rights Act?[31] Congressman Casey responded as follows:

> I will tell the gentleman again, and I will
> repeat what HEW said, and that is that we do not
> care how you do it, but you are going to get a
> certain number of black students in this school,
> and you are going to get a certain number of white
> students in this other school, and you are going
> to get a certain number of white teachers in this
> school.[32]

The ensuing debate was almost identical to that over the 1968 HEW appropriations. The result was also the same, Cohelan's striking amendments lost--141 ayes to 158 nays.

In the Senate, the appropriations committee reported only a slightly modified form of sections 408 and 409. In each section the committee inserted the phrase "to force any school district to take any actions" before the activities intended to be curbed. However, once the bill reached the Senate floor, Senator Scott of Pennsylvania introduced an amendment that would have a far-reaching effect. He called for the insertion of the phrase "Except as required by the Constitution," at the beginning of each section. Senator Scott explained that the amendment ensured against administrative action in derogration of court decisions. Southern Senators argued that the amendment was superfluous in that all acts must be consistent with the Constitution. However, it became clear in the two-day debate that followed that the amendment had the effect, like "racial imbalance," of not blunting school desegregation activities in those areas of the country that formerly enforced segregation by law as distinguished from those areas of the country where segregation was the result of housing patterns combined with the neighborhood school system.

The Minority Leader, Mr. Scott, stated that the Supreme Court decision in Alexander against Holmes County Board of Education--which occurred after the House debate and two months prior to the Senate debate--left no doubt as to the propriety of the Whitten amendments. "Since that decision," said Mr. Scott,

"the President of the United States has declared that his adminis- [33]
tration was committed to enforcing the order of the Supreme Court."
Thus the Whitten amendments would prevent HEW from taking the
course of action that the President had instructed it to take.

Senator Pastore, a co-sponsor of the Scott amendment, added
the following:

> The purpose of the amendment as reported by
> the committee was to create a slowdown that the
> Supreme Court said cannot take place because it
> violates the constitutional rights of the persons
> who are being asked to slow down. [34]

Several Northern Senators said that they were only interested
in stopping forced busing. However, HEW had made an end run around
the prohibition in last year's appropriation bill by stating that any
busing done was for purposes other than correcting racial imbalance.
Senator Dominick believed that the current Whitten amendments were
too broad. They included situations involving busing that had
nothing to do with race.

That race was the crucial point was never in doubt. Yet
Senators from the South saw no difference between de jure segregation and de facto segregation. Before the 1954 Brown decision
de jure segregation was legal. After 1954 it was not legal.
Before 1954 many northern states had school systems practicing de
jure segregation. Senator Stennis declared that it certainly was
not a southern institution. Eight States beyond the South, which
happen to have 91 percent of the Negro school population, at one
time had laws that permitted or required segregation of the races
in the schools. These States included Illinois, New York, Ohio,
Indiana, New Jersey and others. These laws were not repealed until
well into the 20th century and the extreme segregation in those
areas of those States "grew up in exactly the same way that segregation grew up in the South, under its segregation laws," Stennis
said. [35]

Senator Eastland of Mississippi joined Stennis in pointing out
the meaninglessness of the distinction between "de facto" and
"de jure" segregation. "It should not be used to discriminate
against the South," said Eastland. [36] The housing patterns in the
North did not just happen; the law either sanctioned or permitted
their existence and growth.

Mr. Byrd of Virginia reported on December 17 that the state
of New Jersey had been stung by Stennis' charges of the previous
day and that the state had ordered 99 districts to end de facto
segregation within two months.

75

Senator Thurmond of South Carolina siad the Whitten provi-
sions were "in line with the policy of the President of the
United States as expressed by him in Charlotte, N.C., in Anaheim,
Calif., in Washington, D.C., and perhaps in some other places, and
that is free, clear freedom of choice."[37] Senator Ellender of
Louisiana accused the administration of speaking out of both sides
of its mouth on this vital issue. He had earlier joined Senator
Allen in recalling the consideration of the 1964 Civil Rights
Act:

> I can well remember that when the first civil
> rights bill was submitted, the Senator from Illinois
> Mr. Dirksen, opposed it very vehemently until some
> language was inserted in the school desegregation
> section--title IV of the act--to protect the
> State of Illinois and other Northern States from
> the coverage of the law.[38]

Mr. Ervin joined his colleagues from the South in their
assault on the North. He asked Senator Scott if he knew of a
single instance in the State of Pennsylvania in which HEW had
withheld school funds because the schools were all white or black.
The Pennsylvania Senator replied that such action had not been
necessary because "failure to obtain a desired blending of the
situation has occurred for reasons which arise from economic
distribution, from de facto segregation. . . ."[39] Mr. Ervin
responded that the South had had no de jure segregation since
1954.

Despite such protests the Senate voted 52 to 37 to accept
the Scott amendment. On December 18, 1969, the House accepted
a motion by Congressman Conte of Massachusetts that the conferees
on the part of the House be instructed to accept the Scott
amendments to sections 408 and 409. A month later the Senate
agreed to the conference report on the bill and sent it to the
President, who vetoed it on the grounds that it was inflationary.
This action resulted in both bodies going through virtually the
same steps on the new measure as they had on the prior one.
However, this time in the debate on school busing, Southern Senators
picked up a number of Northern colleagues who were motivated either
by "Northern hypocrisy" or troubled by the growing number of court
orders requiring busing. Despite this added support the Senate
incorporated the Scott amendments to the Whitten provisions.

A year after House passage of a three-year extension of the
1965 Elementary and Secondary Education Act (HR 514) on April 23,
1969, Congress finally agreed to the conference report. Prior to
final action, the Senate engaged in two major debates over equal
enforcement throughout the nation of Federal desegregation guide-

lines. The most heated controversy on the bill focused on an
amendment offered by Senator Stennis of Mississippi and Senator
Ribicoff of Connecticut. These two unlikely allies asked that
Federal guidelines on school desegregation be applied equally
to segregation in the North and South, whether de jure or de facto.

The debate lasted from February 4 to February 19 and centered
almost entirely on two Stennis amendments. Amendment No. 481 reads
as follows:

> Sec. 2 (a) No person shall be refused admission
> into or be excluded from any public school in
> any State on account of race, creed, color, or
> national origin
> (b) except with the express approval of a board
> of education legally constituted in any State or
> the District of Columbia and having jurisdiction,
> no student shall be assigned or compelled to attend
> any school on account of race, creed, color, or
> national origin, or for the purpose of achieving
> equality in attendance or increased attendance or
> reduced attendance, at any school of persons of
> one or more particular races, creeds, colors, or
> national origins; and no school district, school
> zone, or attendance unit, by whatever name known,
> shall be established, reorganized, or maintained
> for any such purpose: Provided, That nothing con-
> tained in this Act or any other provision of
> Federal law shall prevent the assignment of a
> pupil in the manner requested or authorized by
> his parents or guardian. [40]

Sixteen of Stennis' Southern colleagues joined him as co-sponsors
of the measure. These Senators joined in a colloquy on the lack
of desegregation enforcement in the North. Of particular interest
to them was a bill passed by the assembly of the State of New York
to end the compulsory busing of school children for the purpose
of integration. Governor Rockefeller signed the bill into law
and it became effective on September 1, 1969.

Debate proceeded along familiar lines until Senator Ribicoff
of Connecticut gained the floor. He announced he would not support
amendment No. 481 even though it was based on a 1969 New York
State law. However, if this amendment failed, he would support
amendment No. 463 which Stennis had promised to bring up. This
amendment would enforce school desegregation uniformly throughout
the Nation, eliminating any legal differences between de facto and
de jure segregation. Ribicoff referred to an HEW report showing

widespread segregation in public schools in both the North and
South. He accused the North of "monumental hypocrisy" in its
treatment of the black man:

> Without question, northern communities have
> been as systematic and as consistent as south-
> ern communities in denying the black man and
> his children the opportunities that exist for
> white people.[41]

The Connecticut Senator went on to say that the dual school system
was not the only problem: "Massive school segregation does not
exist because we have segregated our schools but because we have
segregated our society and our neighborhoods."[42] He suggested a
role for Federal Government that was not built around "ideological
purity" but would lead to "social growth."

Ribicoff was widely praised for his honesty and courage by
Northern liberal and Southern conservative alike. Senator Talmadge
of Georgia pointed out a speech recently given by former Vice-
President Hubert Humphrey at Emory University in Atlanta in which
he declared that orders to desegregate schools "should be applied
nationwide"--not just in the South. Humphrey added that "the
de facto segregation in the North is often more sinister than
the . . . segregation of the South."[43] At the same time, Senator
Talmadge read into the Record two New York Times articles reporting
that school integration had led to widespread racial strife.

Richard Russell of Georgia stated that "this is the first
time that a so-called northern liberal has risen here to ask for
fairness."[44] However, northern liberals Javits and Mondale questioned the usefulness of Ribicoff's position. Javits said that
he wanted to attack "both situations" but the de jure segregation
was easier to act on. He argued that the Constitution and law
prevented him from attacking defacto segregation "as hard as I
would like."[45] While Mondale agreed that actions needed to be
taken in the North, he believed that there was nothing in the
Stennis amendment guaranteeing such action. "Let us not kid ourselves that this does anything about the problem of de facto
segregation. It may simply weaken the effort to do anything
about de jure segregation."[46] Mondale stated that the result
may be the same but different remedies were required. Senator
Pell, chairman of the Education Subcommittee, argued that the
amendment and the debate surrounding it would be more appropriate
in a civil rights bill.

Before Stennis amendment was voted on, Ribicoff succeeded
in adding language specifically mentioning de facto and de jure
segregation. Minority Leader Hugh Scott offered a substitute

amendment which contained the same language except for a stipu-
lation that the policy would deal with "unconstitutional" segregation. While Scott argued that his amendment had Administration
backing, other Republicans argued that the Administration was
neutral in regard to the Stennis amendment. On a roll-call vote
Scott's substitute failed 46 to 48.

On February 18, the Stennis amendment as amended by Ribicoff
to establish as U.S. policy under Title VI of the 1964 Civil
Rights Act and ESEA civil rights provisions that school desegregation passed 56 to 36. Voting in the affirmative were 27 Republicans, 11 northern Democrats and 18 southern Democrats.

Despite the strong Senate stand on this issue the House-
Senate conference reported a bill that significantly changed the
intent of the Stennis-Ribicoff amendment. Added to the original
language was the following subsection:

> Sec. 2 (b) Such uniformity refers to one policy
> applied uniformly to de jure segregation wherever
> found and such other policy as may be provided
> pursuant to law applied uniformly to de facto
> segregation wherever found.[47]

Proponents of the Stennis amendments argued that the new section
segregated segregation. It provided for two rules of uniformity
in relation to two types of segregation instead of one rule of
uniformity for all types of segregation. If segregation was an
evil, they argued, then it should not be classified into types.

The Senate conferees said that the section retained the basic
thrust of the Stennis amendment. House conferees proposed section
2 (b) and were adamantly opposed to the Stennis amendment as it
originally passed the Senate. Under the conference language de
facto segregation would be treated in the same manner throughout
the nation. Senator Eagleton added that there was a fear that
lumping both de facto and de jure segregation together would lead
to a cessation of enforcement activity under Title VI of the
1964 Civil Rights Act. (On the same day, March 24, 1970,
President Nixon issued a comprehensive statement on the subject
of school desegregation that in essence reaffirmed the
distinction between de jure and de facto segregation in regard to
the law.)

Both Stennis and Ribicoff objected that the conference report
was worse than no report at all in regard to their amendment.
In the week of debate that followed the report Stennis said:

> The Nation now has three major school desegre-
> gation policy statements before it--none of which
> wholly agrees with the other.
>
> The Senate has laid down one policy, the Senate-
> House conferees another, and the President still
> another.[48]

The result was a high state of confusion that left every public
official in doubt as to what the law required in relation to
school desegregation, Stennis argued. This confusion left unanswered what he considered the vital question:

> At what point and under what circumstances
> will segregated conditions in the South that
> meet the test of de facto segregation in the
> North be recognized as de facto segregation even
> though that segregation arose in a jurisdiction
> that required segregation by law?[49]

Ribicoff argued that those who opposed de facto segregation
but refused to act until the Supreme Court had spoken were
shirking their responsibility.

> We have come full circle. The Supreme Court
> once was expected to tackle political questions
> only when it was clear that the political process
> was unable or completely unwilling to act. The
> argument now seems to be that Congress will not
> act until the Supreme Court has taken a position.[50]

The arguments of the Connecticut Senator were not persuasive
enough to pass his recommital motion. The motion lost 43 to 32
with 16 Republicans, 4 northern Democrats, and 12 southern
Democrats voting in the affirmative.

Anti-busing forces were also picking-up Northern liberal
support in the House as well as the Senate. Once again anti-
busing forces were defeated when the House voted 164-222 to reject
a motion to kill the proposal that the House accept the weakening
language of the Senate. However, on this second Labor-HEW
appropriations bill (Mr. Nixon vetoed the first for that year),
26 Democrats from the North voted for the proposal to kill the
Senate language.

Roman Pucinski (D-Ill.) was perhaps a sign of things to
come. He was a high-ranking member of the House Education and
Labor Committee and--until 1966--champion of every civil rights
measure which came to the House floor. Yet racial fears in his

predominantly white constituency made his 1966 re-election fight
a close one. Chicago also received a well-publicized federal
warning in regard to its segregated schools. (It will be recalled
that Mayor Daley managed to nullify the threat by going to President Johnson.) In 1970 Pucinski cast his first record vote with
anti-busing forces. By 1971 the Illinois Congressman was one of
the leaders of the anti-busing majority.

This anti-busing majority occurred for the first time in
June of 1970 on a motion which required House conferees on the
education appropriations bill to agree to Senate action dropping
the modified Whitten amendment. The motion was killed, 191-157
with 18 non-southern Democrats joining the anti-busing forces.
Among the non-southern Republicans voting with the majority were
H. Allen Smith of California and William Broomfield of Michigan.
The districts of both these Congressmen had been subject to court
ordered busing plans in the months immediately preceding their
vote.

Although HEW officials said that the Whitten proposals would
have no effect, the House once again refused to cut the amendment
from the education appropriations bill for fiscal 1972. This time
5 more (23) non-southern Democrats voted with the anti-busing
forces. By the time the House voted in November on the anti-busing
amendments to the Higher Education Act of 1971, the uproar in
San Francisco, Pontiac, Detroit, Indianapolis and other urban
and suburban areas was being felt in Congress.

It is most interesting to look at the state delegation voting
pattern on the busing issue. Michigan Representatives voted 15-1
for the Broomfield amendment delaying the effective date of any
court order requiring busing, until all appeals had been acted upon
or the time for them had expired. Six other Michigan Representatives,
including liberals James O'Hara and William Ford, sponsored the
amendment.

Reflecting similar shifts, the delegations of Connecticut,
Illinois, Indiana, New York, Ohio, Pennsylvania and Wisconsin
voted lopsidedly for the amendment. However, the Alabama and
South Carolina delegations split on the Broomfield amendment,
5-3 and 3-3; the Georgia delegation voted against it 1-6.

Southern opposition to the amendment can be seen as retali-
ation for northern hypocrisy on the busing issue. When busing
moved to close to home the northern Representatives immediately
moved to halt it. Jack Edwards of Alabama explained his negative
vote this way:

81

> We are busing all over the 1st District
> of Alabama . . . . A lot of people say to me,
> 'How in the world are we ever going to stop
> this madness?' I say, 'It will stop the day it
> starts taking place across the country, in the
> North, in the East, in the West.'
>
> And so busing is ordered in Michigan and
> the first thing the members from Michigan do
> is come in with this amendment and ask us to
> delay it for them. But, my friends, we are not
> going to stop the busing as long as we let them
> off the hook the minute it hits them. Let it
> hurt them, and we will get their votes as we
> try to stop it once and for all.[51]

The Senate in March 1972 voted to substitute the more moderate
Scott-Mansfield amendment before the Higher Education Amendments
of 1972 went to conference. As a result the House voted on
March 8 to instruct its conferees on the anti-busing amendments.
It was pointed out by proponents of the amendment that at best
4 of 20 House conferees had voted for the Broomfield and
Ashbrook-Green amendments. Congressman Carey of New York suggested
that an issue was being concocted "more with a view to the vote
in the Florida primary than concern for the children of the United
States [President Nixon supported the House amendments]."[52] However, the House reaffirmed this position in May by voting for
the second time to instruct the conferees to insist on the House-
approved anti-busing amendments.

It was reported that the conferees worked principally from
the Ashbrook, Green and Broomfield amendments rather than the
Scott-Mansfield amendment. The Ashbrook Amendment prohibited the
use of any federal education funds for transporting students or
teachers to correct racial imbalance or to achieve desegregation.
The Scott-Mansfield amendment, added when the bill was before
the Senate, limited this prohibition by allowing the funds to
be used for transportation upon the express written request of
local school officials. The Conference committee adopted a version of this amendment close to the Senate version. The Green
amendment prohibited Federal officials: (1) from urging, per-
suading, inducing or requiring any recipient of federal funds
to use state or local funds to transport students or teachers to
correct racial imbalance or achieve desegregation; or (2) to
condition the grant of federal funds upon such use of non-federal
money. The conferees adopted the modified Senate version (Scott-
Mansfield) which added the phrase "unless constitutionally required,"
which would permit a requirement of busing if necessary to eliminate a dual school system. Finally, the Broomfield amendment

82

delayed the effective date of all federal district court orders
requiring the <u>transfer</u> or <u>transportation</u> of students to achieve
racial balance until all appeals had been ruled on, or the time
for them had expired. The Scott-Mansfield amendment limited the
stay to orders involving transportation between school districts
or orders requiring the consolidation of school districts. The
Broomfield amendment prevailed in the Conference committee with
two changes: a phrase limiting its applicability to January 1,
1974; and a clarification of language intended to keep it from
applying retroactively.

Leading off the debate on the conference report, Senator
Griffin of Michigan offered a motion to recommit the report to
conference with instructions to accept the House position on anti-
busing measures. Griffin's motion was defeated but the busing
issue was still the focus of debate even though the busing
amendments were only a small part of the omnibus higher education
measure, which was two years in the making.

Advocates as well as opponents of busing attacked the compromise. Senator Baker of Tennessee, who had offered an amendment to delay busing earlier in the session, asked whether the
conference provision would postpone busing in Nashville, where
a district court order had been handed down but was being appealed.
Senator Pell, floor manager of the bill, said his interpretation
of the compromise was that busing in Nashville would be postponed,
whereupon Baker said he felt he could not support the Griffin
motion to recommit.

Senator Mondale of Minnesota believed the inclusion of the
Broomfield amendment "would represent the first congressional
retreat from the national commitment to nondiscrimination in
public education embodied in the Civil Rights Act of 1964."[53]
Mondale was joined by Javits and Ribicoff in opposing the conference report. Only one southern senator voting, Senator Gambrell
of Georgia, voted against the conference report on the grounds
that the busing provisions were not strong enough. The conference
report was adopted by a roll-call vote of 63 to 15.

Debate on this bill was rather anti-climactic, as it came
two months after President Nixon proposed two new school desegregation measures. <u>The Equal Educational Opportunities Act of 1972</u>
would:

>   --Require that no State or locality could deny
>   equal educational opportunity to any person on
>   account of race, color or national origin.
>   --Establish criteria for determining what con-

stitutes a denial of equal opportunity.
--Establish priorities of remedies for schools
that are required to desegregate, with busing
to be required only as a last resort, and then
only under strict limitations.
--Provide for the concentration of Federal school-
aid funds specifically on the areas of greatest
educational need . . . .[54]

The President's second proposal was The Student Transportation
Moratorium Act of 1972:

--This would provide a period of time during which
any future, new busing orders by the courts would
not go into effect, while Congress considered
legislative approaches--such as the Equal Educational Opportunities Act--to questions raised
by school desegregation cases. This moratorium
on new busing would be effective until July 1,
1973, or until Congress passed the appropriate
legislation, whichever was sooner.[55]

President Nixon concluded his statement by saying that a constitutional amendment would take too long and did not allow for
necessarily detailed prescription.

It was not until October of 1972 that the Senate began
consideration of The Equal Opportunities Act of 1972 (HR 13915).
By that time the bill contained a "reopener clause" that would
allow previously settled desegregation cases to be subjected to
review. In one sense the Chief Executive's legislation completes
a full circle initiated by the Chief Executive in the 1964 Civil
Rights Act. Hubert Humphrey, who had once again returned to the
Senate, pointed out the contradictions involved in the Nixon
Administration's proposal:

What a marvelous irony. What an irony that
today, in 1972, some of those who argue that
section 5 [of the 14th amendment] gives Congress
the power to enact legislation, are the very
same people who told us in 1964 and 1965 that
there was no authority under that section to
enact the Civil Rights Act of 1964 or the
Voting Rights Act of 1965.[56]

The Minnesota Senator stated that section 5 of the 14th amendment had as its purpose the enforcement of the equal protection
of the laws, not the reduction of that protection. Senator
Humphrey then recalled two measures that had been mentioned in

virtually every discussion of busing and school desegregation since their enactment:

> I think most especially about two titles
> in that Civil Rights Act of 1964; title 4, which
> permitted the Attorney General to bring school
> desegregation lawsuits, and title 6, which helped
> desegregation because it made Federal financial
> assistance contingent upon the absence of racial
> discrimination.

> I think about all that those two titles have
> already meant to making America a better place for
> all of us to live--and I wonder, and I truly
> cannot understand, why anyone would want to undo
> such a step forward.

> Yet that is in my judgment exactly what
> H.R. 13915 is designed to do and would do.[57]

Senator Humphrey's analysis of the Nixon Administration's position on the busing issue is instructive. If Humphrey could not understand federal policy in regard to desegregation, then it was practically impossible for those outside of Washington to understand or carry out such policies. It was the Minnesota Senator who defined the Johnson Administration's position on the 1964 Civil Rights Act. Humphrey's exchange with Robert Byrd was the most frequently mentioned definition of the intent of Title VI in the history of the busing debate. In addition, federal courts have increasingly tended to weigh committee reports and floor debates in interpreting laws.

According to Humphrey, the Johnson Administration regarded Title VI merely as a recognition of the Commissioner's authority to require some gradual plan of integration as a condition for continued Federal aid. While "discrimination" was not defined in Title VI, the Administration assumed that the title forbade only that discrimination found unconstitutional by the courts. However, Senator John Pastore, to whom Humphrey had assigned the more detailed defense of the title, put forward a more forceful and immediate interpretation of its effect. Pastore believed the Brown v. Topeka Board of Education decision meant that school segregation was "absolutely wrong" and Title VI would end the use of the "common wealth of the people of the United States to promote . . . that kind of system." Separate school systems would be eliminated "once and for all."[58]

By contrast, Humphrey was seeking to reassure Senator Byrd that President Johnson would reject any "racial balance" require-

ment. Humphrey was supported by Senator Javits who said that any
school district ordered to bus could easily get a court order
to release federal funds. Yet the courts were to become the
ultimate instrument through which busing was accomplished.

Despite Humphrey's compromises with Minority Leader Everett
Dirksen, who was concerned about Federal regulation of northern
school practices, the Minnesota Senator did leave an opening for
future regulation of northern school systems in which the courts
found unconstitutional segregation. This was done by defining
Title VI in relationship to judicial interpretations of the
Constitution. Thus it left open the possibility that evolution
of constitutional law would expand the Federal requirement and
that is precisely what happened.

In 1966, the Fifth Circuit Court of Appeals focused on the
school system as a whole and said that formerly dual systems had
to convert to "unitary" or single systems without racial division.
Freedom-of-choice plans would be acceptable only if they resulted
in desegregation, and not merely in the possibility of desegregation.
The Green decision took the burden of "free choice" off the student and placed it on the school board. The impact of the decision is reflected in the number of local school boards asking for
assistance in formulating desegregation plans. In 1967, the
Office of Education received 1400 requests and produced 12 desegregation plans. By 1968 the requests had risen to 4000 with a response of 411 plans and the first half of 1969 totaled 2487 requests
and 517 desegregation plans.[59] The court action also had the
effect of reducing the political pressure on the Commissioner
of Education, Harold Howe, II. Prior to these decisions both the
House Rules Committee and the House Judiciary Committee had investi-
gated Howe's administration which had actively carried out the
law. In fact, Howe's actions were responsible for Title VI's
authority being transferred from the Office of Education to the
Office of the HEW secretary.[60]

The final area of "constitutional expansion" in regard to
school desegregation came in 1971 in the case of Swann v.
Charlotte-Mecklenburg Board of Education. In this case the
Supreme Court finally attacked the issue of de facto segregation.
In the rural areas of the South, school desegregation had involved
little busing because many blacks and whites lived interspersed.
However, the urban centers, both North and South posed a different
problem. In an opinion written by Nixon-appointed Chief Justice
Warren Burger, the Court unanimously ruled that all things being
equal it was desirable to assign pupils to neighborhood schools
but all "things are not equal in a system that has been deliberately
constructed and maintained to enforce racial segregation." It
was not enough now for such a community to come forward with a

86

"racially neutral" assignment plan based on existing residential
patterns that in themselves had developed around segregated schools
in the past, because "such plans may fail to counteract the continuing effects of past school segregation resulting from discriminatory location of school sites or distortion of school size
in order to achieve or maintain an artificial racial separation." [61]
Two years later the Court put the North and West on notice with
its decision in Keyes v. Denver School District No. 1 which once
again ordered the district to go beyond providing racially neutral
assignment plans for the future.

The Court seemed to accept the Stennis argument that northern
states had practiced de jure segregation prior to the decision in
Brown. However, in Swann the Court was going further than it had
in Brown which spoke only of "racial discrimination" and not
against "segregation." In fact, in making the Brown decision the
historical evidence seemed to demonstrate that neither Congress
in drawing up the Fourteenth Amendment nor the state legislatures
which adopted it understood it as requiring the end of segregation
in the nation's public schools. Passage of the amendment caused
little discussion of Jim Crow schools despite the existence of
such schools in twenty-four of the thirty-seven states in the
Union.[62] While the Warren Court concluded that conditions had
changed in intervening years, the Brown decision was not nearly
as bold as Swann.

With Swann the Burger Court, despite Congressional and
Presidential opposition, took a major step in eliminating the
distinction between de jure and de facto segregation.[63] Like
Senator Ribicoff, normative beliefs and cognitive knowledge have
come together on the issue of race. Yet the Court's opinion may
have only symbolic effect until it, like Brown, is supported by
other governmental policy-makers. Such support may be slow in
coming as long as confusing terms like liberal, conservative,
integration and racial balance abound.64

Our discussion has illustrated that important historical
differences between the North and the South have led to different
cognitions and normative values in regard to racial issues.
While governmental policy from the Roberts decision through Brown
attempted to demonstrate its geographic, if not racial fairness,
it merely demonstrated the cultural myopia of the nation's policy-
makers. Blacks, on the other hand, have often placed too much
faith in the symbolic significance of governmental policies without looking for their substantive impact. Busing, as racial
governmental policy, is a cue to group status but may or may not
have anything to do with "quality education."

87

In racial governmental policy with substantive content, the
cultural ambiquity of governmental policy promises to have profound impact. Affirmative action programs, minority business
programs, mental health training grants programs, and public works
statutes are among the areas in which this policy becomes visible.
The most significant challenge to date is the Regents of the
University of California v. Bakke. In this case the constitutionality of a special admissions program used by the medical school
at the Davis campus of the University of California to insure
the enrollment of a representative number of minority students
has been challenged by a 37-year old white engineer--Allan Bakke,
who was twice denied admission.

Mr. Bakke's case is illuminating for a number of reasons.
Bakke is not claiming that he was denied admission because of his
religion or national origin but because he is white. If one
accepts DuBois' notion that racial separation has variable significance, then it is far-fetched to argue that the purpose of the
university's admissions program is the subjugation or oppression
of whites.

Although the medical school at Davis is a new one, only a
severe case of myopia could prevent one from seeing rampant racial
discrimination in the University of California's history. During
the period from the end of the Civil War to the beginning of
World War II, only one black graduated from the university's
medical school in San Francisco. At Davis, blacks were once
prohibited from living on campus. Yet none of this information
was part of the trial record in the lower court. Moreover, the
Justice Department's friend-of-the-court brief in the Bakke case
cites a number of other omissions in the findings of the trial
court. Among them was the question of why the particular target
of 16 positions was selected and whether the number was flexible
or not. In addition, it is not clear from the record why Asian-
American persons are included in the special program. While
Asian-Americans are certainly a minority, the available evidence
suggests that they are admitted in substantial numbers even
without the help of special admissions. The Medical School,
which lost the case in the Supreme Court of California, argued
that minority physicians serving minority communities was a noble
goal; it did not address the question of how race was used and why.

The fate of Mr. Bakke may hinge on Title VI of the Civil
Rights Act of 1964. The University of California and the Department
of Justice have argued that Title VI supports the use of special
admissions programs for members of minority groups. Mr. Bakke's
lawyer has told the Court that Title VI provides "no group rights,"
since it says "no person" shall be discriminated against on

grounds of race, religion, or national origin in a federally
aided education program.

Our discussion of Title VI of the 1964 Civil Rights Act would
appear to give the Court the flexibility to rule either way.
Senator Humphrey left the door open regarding the future regulation
of northern school systems in which the courts found unconstitutional segregation. By defining Title VI in relationship to
judicial interpretations of the Constitution, it is possible to
expand the federal role to include more than racial neutrality.
However, it seems obvious that both public and private racial
policy that does not include a cultural component is likely to
be rigid and subject to contradiction. Such policy serves neither
majority nor minority interests.

General Attitudes on Integration   (N=2006)
and Busing*

	Support	Oppose	No Opinion	Totals
Integration as a national objective	67%	22%	11%	100%
General support for busing	21%	70%	9%	100%

TABLE 2

Attitudes of Integration Supporters and Opponents on General Busing
Question   (N=2006)

	Support Busing	Oppose Busing	No Opinion	Totals
Integration supporters	27%	67%	6%	100%
Integration opponents	9%	87%	4%	100%

U.S. Civil Rights Commission national poll.   March 1972.

TABLE 8-7 Estimated Percentage of White and Negro Households Located
in 1967 in Integrated and Segregated Neighborhoods in the United States

RACIAL CHARACTERISTICS OF HOUSEHOLD AND NEIGHBORHOOD		GEOGRAPHIC AREA		
	In total U.S.	In all metropolitan areas	In central cities of those metropolitan areas	In suburbs of those metropolitan areas
Percentages of White Households				
In integrated neighborhoods	19.6	22.8	33.0	16.6
Characterized as "open"[1]	6.1	9.1	11.5	5.0
Characterized as "integrating"[2]	4.5	6.6	9.5	4.8
Characterized as "substantially integrated"[3]	2.4	3.3	5.2	2.1
Other[4]	6.6	3.8	6.8	1.7
In segregated neighborhoods	80.4	77.2	67.0	83.4
Percentage of Negro Households				
In integrated neighborhoods	13.6	15.0	10.9	12.7
Characterized as "open"	0.1	0.1	0.1	0.2
Characterized as "integrating"	0.9	1.2	0.5	2.5
Characterized as "substantially integrated"	8.9	12.7	9.5	9.6
Other	3.7	1.0	0.9	0.4
In segregated neighborhoods	86.4	85.0	89.1	87.3
Percentage of All Households				
In integrated neighborhoods	19.0	22.0	28.2	16.4
Characterized as "open"	5.5	8.3	9.0	7.6
Characterized as "integrating"	4.2	6.1	7.5	4.7
Characterized as "substantially integrated"	3.0	4.1	6.2	2.4
Other	6.3	3.5	5.5	1.7
In segregated neighborhoods	81.0	78.0	71.8	83.6

SOURCE: Sudman, Bradburn, and Gockel, "The Extent and Characteristics of
Racially Integrated Housing in the United States," *The Journal of Business of
the University of Chicago*, January, 1969.

APPENDIX III.

Statistical tables below show the pace of desegregation for the nation, the 11 Southern states, the 6 border states and the District of Columbia, and the 32 Northern and Western states, in terms of blacks in majority white schools, and blacks in all-black schools.

BLACKS IN MAJORITY WHITE SCHOOLS

	U. S.	South	Border & D.C.	North & West
1968-69	23.4%	18.4%	28.4%	27.6%
1970-71	33.1%	40.3%	28.7%	27.6%
1972-73	36.3%	46.3%	31.8%	28.3%

BLACKS IN ALL-BLACK SCHOOLS

	U. S.	South	Border & D.C.	North & West
1958-69	39.7%	68.0%	25.2%	12.3%
1970-71	14.0%	14.4%	24.1%	11.7%
1972-73	11.2%	8.7%	23.6%	10.9%

SCHOOL DESEGREGATION 1954-74
Blacks in Schools with Whites
11 Southern States

1954-55	.001%	1964-65	2.25%
1955-56	.115%	1965-66	6.1 %
1956-57	.144%	1966-67	15.9 %
1957-58	.151%	1967-68	NA
1958-59	.132%	1968-69	32.0 %
1959-60	.160%	1969-70	NA

SCHOOL DESEGREGATION 1954-74
Blacks in Schools with Whites
11 Southern States

1960-61	.162%	1970-71	85.6%
1961-62	.241%	1971-72	90.8%
1962-63	.453%	1972-73	91.3%
1963-64	1.17%	1973-74	NA

Source: Lou Mathis, Chief of Public Affairs
Office for Civil Rights
Department of Health, Education and Welfare
330 Independence Avenue, S.W.
Washington, D.C. 20021
Telephone: 202/245-6671

CHAPTER III
FOOTNOTES

Part II

[1]See Herbert Hirsch and Lewis Donohew, "A Note on Negro-White Differences in Attitudes Toward the Supreme Court" _Social Science Quarterly_, 49, 3 (Dec., 1968), p. 562.

[2]Wallace Mendelson, "Judicial Review and Party Politics" _Vanderbilt Law Review_, Vol. 12, (March, 1959) p. 447.

[3]Robert A. Dahl, "Decision-Making in a Democracy: The Supreme Court as a National Policy-Maker" _Journal of Public Law_, 6 (Fall, 1957), pp. 279-295.

[4]Jonathan D. Casper, "The Supreme Court and National Policy Making" _American Political Science Review_, Vol. LXX (March, 1976), pp. 50-63.

[5]Stanley Fleishman and Sam Rosenwein, _The New Civil Rights Act_, (Los Angeles: Blackstone, 1964), p. 119.

[6]Senator Hubert Humphrey as quoted in Raymond J. Calada, _Federal Anti-Busing Provisions: A Legislative History_, (Washington, D.C.: Congressional Research Service, March 17, 1970), p. vi.

[7]Ibid

[8]See addition

[9]_Congressional Record_, 1 February 1964, p. H 1598.

[10]_Congressional Record_, 6 October 1966, p. H 25549.

[11]Ibid., p. H 25551.

[12]Senator Robert Byrd as quoted in Celada, _Federal Anti-Busing Provisions: A Legislative History_, p. 23.

[13]_Congressional Record_, 2 August 1976, p. S 21001.

[14]Judge Skelly Wright as quoted in Celada, _Federal Anti-Busing Provisions: A Legislative History_, pp. 25-26.

[15]_Congressional Record_, 8 November 1967, p. S 31677.

94

[16] Senator Dirksen's amendment as quoted in Celada, Federal Anti-Busing Provisions: A Legislative History, p. 33.

[17] Senator Dirksen as quoted in Celada, Federal Anti-Busing Provisions: A Legislative History, p. 33.

[18] Congressional Record, 4 December 1967, p. S 24965.

[19] Ibid., pp. S 34965-34966.

[20] Congressional Record, 5 December 1967, p. S 35082.

[21] Congressional Record, 5 December 1967, p. S 34976.

[22] Provisions of H.R. 180374, 90th Congress, 2nd session as quoted in Celada, Federal Anti-Busing Provisions: A Legislative History, p. 64.

[23] Congressional Record, 26 June 1968, p. H 18925.

[24] Ibid., p. H 18926.

[25] Ibid.

[26] Ibid., p. H 18927.

[27] Congressional Record, 26 June 1968, p. H 18932.

[28] Ibid., p. J 18933.

[29] Congressional Record, 3 October 1968, p. H 29444.

[30] Congressional Record, 31 July 1969, p. H 6625.

[31] Ibid., p. H 6626

[32] Ibid.

[33] Congressional Record, 16 December 1969, p. S 16898.

[34] Ibid., p. S 16899.

[35] Ibid., pp. S 16902, 16903.

[36] Ibid., p. S 16915.

[37] Congressional Record, 17 December 1969, p. S 16952.

[38] Ibid., p. S 16953.

[39] Ibid., p. 16959.

[40] Congressional Record, 5 February 1970, p. S 2547.

[41] Congressional Record, 9 February 1970, p. S 2892.

[42] Ibid.

[43] Ibid., p. S 2894.

[44] Ibid., p. S 2902.

[45] Ibid., p. S 2901.

[46] Ibid., p. S 2904.

[47] Congressional Record, 24 March 1970, p. S 8851.

[48] Congressional Record, 1 April 1970, p. S 10000.

[49] Ibid., p. S 10002.

[50] Ibid., p. S 10015.

[51] Congressional Record, 8 March 1972, p. H 1842.

[52] Ibid., p. H 1847.

[53] Congressional Record, 24 May 1972, p. S 8386.

[54] Office of the White House Press Secretary, Press Release on "The Equal Educational Opportunities Act of 1972," 17 March 1972, pp. 2-3.

[55] Ibid., p. 3

[56] Congressional Record, 10 October 1972, p. S 17349.

[57] Ibid.

[58] Orfield, The Reconstruction of Southern Education: The Schools and the 1964 Civil Rights Act, p.42.

[59] Interview with Gregory Anrig (former director of Equal Opportunities Division of HEW) Civil Rights Documentation Project, Howard University, October 24, 1969, p. 23.

[60] Ibid., p. 3-4.

[61]Richard Kluger, Simple Justice, p. 767.

[62]Ibid., pp. 627-635 for the Congressional debate surrounding the Fourteenth Amendment.

[63]Former HEW Secretary John Gardner believed de facto segregation was just as damaging as de jure (Elaine Heffernan Interview in CRDP 9/19/69). Former Attorney-General Ramsey Clark states that "there is no de facto segregation...All segregation reflects some past actions of our governments (FHA loans for example)..." (Clark quoted in Nathan Glazer "is Busing Necessary?" Commentary, March, 1972, p. 44.

[64]Thomas Pettigrew states that "Desegregation involves only a specification of the racial mix of students--preferably, more than half white (physical orientation). It does not include any description of the quality of the interracial acceptance (cultural orientation). See Pettigrew "Race and Equal Educational Opportunity" Harvard Education Review, Winter 1968, p. 71. A U.S. Civil Rights Commission poll finds that two-thirds of the people who say they support integration are also generally opposed to busing. See Appendix.

CHAPTER IV

Ideological Conflict and Misunderstanding
on the Local Level: Community Control As
Nationalist and Integrationist

Perhaps what is considered a simple problem of composition
or style of expression, can reflect the complex methodological
problems one faces in attempting to state an issue precisely.
At least this was the case in setting up the present analysis
of the conflict in New York City's Ocean Hill-Brownsville, which
gained national prominence through the teachers strikes of 1968.
To identify the situation as simply a teachers strike seemed to
predispose the argument to the claims of the United Federation
of Teachers that "the real issue" centered around "due process"
or "jobs". On the other hand, to use the title of "community
control" seemed to reflect the attitude of the Ocean Hill-
Brownsville officials, who held that community and racial self-
determination were at issue. Participants in the conflict were
also very sensitive to the influence that a name for the events
might have (not to mention their apparent interest in name-calling).
As such, a secondary division of participants has developed which
conforms to the attitudes and opinions held by the two major groups
in the conflict.

It is therefore fitting to apply content analysis to the
statements of participants in order to identify the focus of
opinion variation. Content analysis can be more productive here
than in other chapters because the political and cultural range
of the events is more rigidly confined by other factors. These
events took place in a single urban community in approximately
one year and involved primarily those who had been previously
involved in public education. In particular, the specification
of an educational establishment creates a culturally uniform set
of objects and concepts around which attitudinal as well as
secondary conceptual variation can be gauged. Unfortunately, the
size and number of direct statements from participants is not

sufficient to allow a very rigid form of content analysis. However, an abbreviated form[1], used here, is adequate to make some accurate and useful distinctions.

History-1968

The sequence of events through which the school conflict evolved can only loosely be called history in that the tensions, polarizations, and reactions are still manifesting themselves. However, the present analysis is not concerned with the events themselves but rather with the feelings or dispositions of the participants to which the events are related as both cause and effect. In this respect, only a brief sketch of the history is necessary.

The Ocean Hill-Brownsville governing board with its constituents and the United Federation of Teachers represent the primary actors and conflict groups. The central Board of Education of the city, Superintendent of Schools Donovan, Mayor Lindsay, State Education Commissioner Allen and others played prominent but non-pivotal roles in the conflict. That is to say, the essential divergence of opinion was between the Ocean Hill-Brownsville group and the U. F. T.; this issue was only dependent on the actions of the city and state officials to the extent that they set the stage and later reappeared after the action had been disrupted.

The Ocean Hill complex consisted of a twenty-four member governing board, led by Rev. C. Herbert Oliver; the district administrator, Rhody McCoy; and district residents and teachers. Because there were only a few dissidents in the group, and these generally did not articulate their views, we are justified in looking at this group as a unified opinion holder.

The U. F. T., consisting of 57,000 teachers, was generally represented by its president, Albert Shanker. Fred Nauman, the Union's Ocean Hill district chairman, was an occasional spokesman. The Council of Supervisory Associations and others played supporting roles. The background of the U. F. T. begins in 1961 when it evolved from the now defunct Teachers Guild which had split from the Teachers Union in 1935. It is worth noting that the evolution of the teachers' organizations has a distinctly political coloring. The Guild separated from the teachers union in order to express a strongly anti-Communist position.[2]

The singularly visible characteristic that distinguishes the opposing groups is race. The Ocean Hill-Brownsville group was largely, though not wholly, black with some Puerto Rican participation. The U. F. T. is virtually all white (with a Jewish majority). Those black teachers (less than ten percent of city

99

teachers), including Union members, who spoke out were opposed
to the Union position.

With such perceptible evidence of polarization by racial
groups, it was probably inevitable that accusations of "racism"
would be made, and probably just as likely that some accusations
would be well-founded. However, there is no attempt, here, to
document the presence or absence of racist attitudes, since these
may be considered the normative containers in which the policy
dispute was conducted. Without racism, the concept and execution
of both policy positions was quite feasible, and secondly, at
least some of the participants on both sides were virtually free
of racism. Keep in mind, however, that the concept of race held
by the participants had to be central, since the racial identity
of the participants was both salient and essential to the events
which precipitated the crisis.

Formal decentralization proposals for the school system
were developed in the summer and fall of 1967 by an advisory
committee to Mayor Lindsay for three experimental school districts
of which the Ocean Hill-Brownsville district was the largest.
The committee was headed by McGeorge Bundy of the Ford Foundation,
and it was the foundation which funded the decentralization project. The plan received much of its impetus from an Ocean Hill
community group seeking more "community control" of schools.
Father Powis, later a member of the governing board, is recognized
as a central figure in this organization.[3] Legislation to
institutionalize school decentralization was being sought coter-
minously in the state government. It culminated after the three
teachers' strikes in the establishment of larger units than the
plan had anticipated. The U. F. T. constituted a major part of
the opposition to the decentralization plan in the legislative
lobby.

The governing board came into being in the fall of 1967
with a membership representing various social positions and based
on varied selection techniques. From each of the eight schools
in the district one parent and one teacher were elected. A
relatively small minority of the community residents participated
in the election, a fact which served as a basis for complaint
during the school crisis, although it was decided in court that
the election had been fair. Five community representatives were
also elected to the board by its parent component. These members, in turn, chose two representatives from among the school
supervisors (principals, assistants, etc.) and one university
delegate. Possibly, the most extraordinary aspect of these
elections, in the sense of attracting public attention, was the
inclusion of several welfare-recipient mothers on the board

100

(a practice which may have gained wider acceptance in subsequent years).

In the process of establishing administrative procedures the board encountered some noteworthy difficulties prior to the strikes. The central board failed to supply the expected list of parents eligible to take part in the elections, which might explain the low turnout. There were delays of many weeks in getting office supplies and telephones. Files, typewriters, etc. were removed from their offices. The U. F. T., joining with the Council of Supervisory Associations, brought suit, seeking "to declare illegal the appointment of four principals whom the governing board had recently chosen to run its schools."[4] The U. F. T. group lost in appeals court.

The brief history of the district also strayed from the commonplace through the numerous steps it took toward educational innovation. It began developing new programs in reading, math, Black and Puerto Rican culture and "bilingualism." Rhody McCoy instituted training programs for "paraprofessionals," who were largely mothers of students whose jobs would be as teacher assistants when they finished training. He also planned for programmed instruction, teaching teams, and non-graded classrooms.[5]

Smoke began to rise from this rather small, poverty-ridden district about May 7, 1968, when Rhody McCoy sent letters to nineteen teachers "transferring" them out of the district. For what it is worth, many claim that the fire had been kindled by student protest and disturbances following the April assassination of Martin Luther King, Jr.[6] Martin Mayer maintains in his book, along with the U. F. T., that the teachers had been fired, presumably as a result of lingering racial hostility.[7] However, this reference must be considered as questionable, if not inaccurate, because, as Jason Epstein points out, the letters to the teachers ordered them to the central board to be "reassigned."[8] The position of the Ocean Hill group that these were simply routine transfers of teachers who were considered unsatisfactory was supported by an investigation of the New York Civil Liberties Union.[9] Still, it should be remembered that it is not so much to our purpose to decide upon the truth of these observations as it is to discern the affective orientations toward the policy alternatives, and the cognitive orientation toward the race-policy-making latent in the dispute.

Subsequent to the transfers, about 200 union teachers in the district, out of about 550 teachers, went on strike. Superintendent of Schools Donovan ordered Rhody McCoy to reinstate the teachers. He refused, excluding one teacher, the only black among the nineteen, who had been reinstated almost immediately. Union teachers demanded that charges be brought against the transferred teachers. The issue was submitted to arbitration under Judge Rivers, retired, who decided to return all six teachers against whom McCoy brought formal charges. It should be noted that this decision was highly criticized, even by some on the Union's side.[10] In the following meticulously worded statement Rev. O. Herbert Oliver, chairman of the governing board, conceded to the decision:

> Since the legal machinery of this sick society are forcing these teachers on us under the threat of closing our schools* and dissolving this district, the Board of Education should return to our district any of the teachers who wish to return. Our original decision remains as before. We refuse to sell out. If the Board of Education and the Superintendent of Schools forces them to return to a community who does not want them, so be it.

Saying that he did not trust the Ocean Hill administration to treat the teachers as it should, Albert Shanker rejected this concession and headed a city-wide strike which began two days later with the September 9 opening of schools. State Commissioner Allen was called in, and he produced a "settlement"--an agreement between Shanker and the Board of Education excluding the Ocean Hill group.[11] The agreement brought the teachers back to work but completely dismissed the governing board. Yet, within a few days, Allen found it necessary to reinstate the board. Subsequently, 50,000 of the 57,000 city teachers were called on strike by Shanker (8,000 teachers participated in the strike vote).[12] This time they stayed out for five weeks, beginning October 14. When the strike was over Ocean Hill-Brownsville, under the terms of the strike settlement, had been placed under state trusteeship. The governing board was retained but it lost most of its appointees as school principals, as well as its right to transfer teachers.

Attitude Objects

We may view an individual's orientation or disposition toward objects, facts or events that he experiences in several ways. An

---

*Mayor Lindsay had started to close J.H.S. 271, a district school which had been involved in civil disturbances.

individual has cognitive, affective, and evaluational orientations.[13] Commonsensically, these may be viewed as conceptual ideals of knowing, feeling and evaluating, respectively. In the study of attitudes we are directly concerned with the latter two, though it is necessary to say something about all three.

The attitudes we wish to discern are those of the U. F. T. and the Ocean Hill group towards the objects most often referred to during the strike. These objects are, broadly speaking, decentralization and job security, or due process in employment. Secondly, after dealing with the more salient and specific aspects of the conflict, we can more easily expose the race-related conceptual conflict which surfaced only vicariously in the altercation over "racism". The concept of due process, abbreviated as jobs, has, it is believed, through extended academic and practical application been sufficiently explicated for the reader to have a relatively clear understanding of the references which will be made to it. The former term, decentralization, has diffuse popular uses and, therefore, demands some explication. One of the referents of decentralization, "community control," is itself rather broad and, as such, should be explicated separately. These can be understood within the setting of New York City educational bureaucracy. The following definitions are a step toward that explication.[14] These definitions are proposed in order to indicate useful distinctions among the governmental procedures around which volatile feelings revolved.

Administrative decentralization refers to the organizational structure "within" the educational bureaucracy. It is a hierarchical form of official relationships in which final authority over all decisions resides at the top, in this case the central Board of Education. Action taken by the lower echelon officers must conform to general guidelines. Routine decisions may be made independently. If a decision is deemed fundamental, it is subject to the central authority as a matter of course. In this kind of system, personnel are employed, directly or indirectly, through the central office. The system may not be closed, in that persons other than those who have recognized offices may be members; for example the mayor may be considered part of the educational bureaucracy.

Administration will be called decentralized when it groups lower echelon offices and responsibilities into sub-groups which mediate between the bureaucratic head and its lowest operatives. In this case, the range of applications or interpretations a sub-group (say Ocean Hill) could give to a policy would be greater than the freedom allowed smaller, individual units.

Decentralization may take place either on a functional or geographic basis. Functional administrative decentralization occurs where the subsidiary units are distinguished on the basis of the scope of their operations. That is to say, each sub-unit has special capabilities and responsibilities with respect to the substantive concerns or "products" of the bureaucracy. In geographical administrative decentralization each unit executes the same kind of operations over separate communities or different groups of people. These two forms are not mutually exclusive.

Political decentralization refers to separate administrative agencies which operate independently of each other although they may have the same substantive concerns, e.g. education. This kind of decentralization is illustrated by the overall system of American government. In the system the sub-units initiate broad policy and have independent authority in the sense that their legitimacy,[15] sociological or de jure, rests on separate constituencies or laws. Political decentralization is functional when interest groups or relatively independent agencies determine policy in a given substantive area. It is geographic when an agency controls policy in a spatial area. Finally, it is complete political decentralization when an agency controls policy in a given substantive and physical area.

Community control in this analysis, and therefore probably in its most consistent popular usage, refers to complete political decentralization. Community control in Ocean Hill-Brownsville education is functional and geographic (it may also be racial, or rather cultural). Race seems to subsume the other distinctions in decentralization. Yet, it can be viewed for the moment as a spurious variable, although it will be hypothesized that race is related in a causal way to feelings about community control.

These conceptual distinctions, or similar ones, are useful if not essential in understanding the various opinions expressed in the school crisis. Statements made by Shanker and McCoy often contained the same words, clearly meant in different ways. This difference in meaning reflects a variation in the cognitive orientations, which it is necessary to recognize, in order to understand the difference in attitudes.

Attitudinal Expressions

Without a highly systematic method of analyzing the content of language, we are largely bound by the manifest content of statements. Fortunately, the limits of the present discussion do not go much beyond this. We do not wish to speak of the total "psychology," ideological framework, or belief-system of either

104

of the two groups, but only an aspect of their belief-systems.

Decentralization(s) and jobs have been selected as the focal points of the content analysis because they seem to be the main issues in the altercation between the U. F. T. and the Ocean Hill group. Unfortunately we cannot analyze policy statements for content to determine a latent concept, like race, when, as argued earlier, the same words conceal multiple conceptual variation. If content analysis were provided a means of imputing a broad (cultural) context to word-meanings, it could then be applied to the concern over race. While contextual word analysis is just as conceivable statistically, it must still depend on a prior definition of the cultural context and/or conceptual alternatives in which we are now engaged. The question then becomes, with respect to the two obvious issues, which one was most important to the participants during the conflict?

In an attempt to answer this question, public statements by both groups have been reviewed. All statements were taken from the New York Times newspaper editions during the crucial months of the conflict, May 1968 through January 9, 1969. Only direct quotes were analyzed. Only those articles were used for content analysis which contained relatively lengthy quotes by the participants--that is, five sentences or more.

There are some apparent difficulties in this approach. First, newspapers are loosely selective in including material. Newspapers, even the New York Times, are considered to be sensationalistic. They may also misrepresent and distort information. Thus there is an uncontrolled bias brought into the procedure. However, by using quotes of some length the probability of editorial distortion is notably reduced.

Sentences in these statements have been reduced to simple sentences containing a subject, predicate and, in some cases, a direct object. The reduction process hopefully decreases confusion by separating out independent assertions according to their cognitive referents. Simplified sentences serve the purpose of "atomic" themes or images.[16] This purpose is to clarify the process of inference, to clarify the meaning attributed to words. In this way, it facilitates interpretation of statements to be examined, and makes it easier for the reader (see appendix) to check or re-evaluate the conclusions of this study.[17]

The evidence thus obtained clearly indicates that the issue of decentralization superceded job security in the conflict between the U. F. T. and Ocean Hill. Although Shanker insisted on numerous occasions that the real issue was due process for teachers, the

consistent references by both parties to decentralization indicates
their major focus. While the sample of statements is small, the
continuity is striking. Only four references from the U. F. T.,
twenty-seven percent, out of fifteen were made to job security.
All thirteen of the references found for Ocean Hill concerned
decentralization.

If decentralization was not the more prominent issue, then
why was it the most discussed? Indeed, with a consistent meaning
for issue, it could hardly be otherwise, unless the question of
job security is too subtle to be brought to the forefront, which
it does not seem to be. Unlike racism, due process in employment
is generally not too volatile to bear the strains of social confrontation.

In fact, the Ocean Hill group viewed the whole due process
question as distortion for the purpose of U. F. T. propaganda.
Correspondingly, the U. F. T. did not make the same kind of
assertions about the decentralization question. In principle,
that was virtually impossible because the union had shown through
its legal suits its interest in the structure of the educational
system. William Kunstler, attorney for the governing board,
observed. "There is absolutely no due process now in the law
regarding involuntary transfers [references McCoy's transfer of
teachers]. The whole due process thing is a myth."

On the other hand, it can be argued that people actually do
raise issues in a frequency inverse to their concerns. To deal
with this scepticism, we shall investigate the strength of feelings
or attitudes on decentralization for each party and see how widely
they diverge. Yet, this procedure cannot show that job security
was of no consequence. Indeed, this analysis has already recognized that jobs were important but secondary. The essential conflict of beliefs, or principle, if you will, involved the structure
of educational authority.

Shortly after the school crisis had subsided both Shanker and
McCoy published articles in the New York Times stating their
positions on decentralization.[18] Interestingly, Shanker says that
with certain "safeguards" decentralization can proceed. Thus, it
might appear that the difference between the two positions was one
of degree rather than kind. Referring to the conceptual distinctions in forms of decentralization, made above, one does not have
to go far to see that Shanker and McCoy were not talking about the
same thing when they used the word in a favorable context. In
essence, the safeguards that Shanker had in mind were barriers
against what Ocean Hill wanted. In qualitative analysis, therefore, we need no methodological yardstick to measure the divergence. Instead, we need to identify the separate concepts and

106

demonstrate their incompatibility.

The relatively peaceful environment upon which the school crisis intruded had already been decentralized long before the Ocean Hill governing board came into existence. Obviously, for example, American politics is decentralized along national, state and local lines by the constitutional framework. This is geographic political decentralization. It is also apparent that the local government is divided among several administrative agencies in New York City. Within the educational system, which notably includes the Board of Education and the Supervisor of Schools, there rests considerable authority to determine the substance and procedure of education. Thus, the City's educational system is a unit in a functionally decentralized political structure.

What needs to be recognized is that New York education has always been still further decentralized along functional lines. Separate "interest groups" have been subtly granted or have assumed power in the running of the schools. The U. F. T. is one of the major interest groups to have such power. This is functional administrative decentralization.

Theodore Lowi, speaking of the power distribution in New York City in his book At the Pleasure of the Mayor, maintained: "Functional specialization of officials and governmental activities has subordinated 'widely shared community values to the special interests of the separate and numerous 'islands of power' within it.'"[19] Lowi's analysis suggests that the U. F. T. was only for decentralization when it meant interest-group power in administration (perhaps also interest-group power in broad politics) but not when it meant community power.

Accordingly, in his most thorough statement on decentralization Shanker shows his concern that it be limited to the administration. He says, "we favor it" for reasons other than those given by the governing board. "First, it is obvious that any large organization, whether in industry or government, can not make all decisions centrally but must delegate decision-making power." He adds, "it [decentralization] can provide for administrative efficiency and flexibility." [20] He also asserts that large districts are much better than small districts because they could be integrated and thus would reduce the chance of "takeover by small extremists groups." These "extremists," he says, "would use public funds to advance discord and [for] the creation of huge community pork-barrel." Statements like these show that Shanker feared the devolution of authority to communities, at least certain communities.

107

Community control, as defined earlier, is a form of political decentralization that is both functional and geographic. In New York such community control could operate partly, but not wholly, within the City's educational bureaucracy. This seemed to be the view of Rhody McCoy when he spoke of Ocean Hill-Brownsville as a structural unit: "We have begun to see the transformation of a community from powerlessness to potency and from inconsequence to relevance in the mainstream of mankind."[21] The mainstream of mankind could only refer to society's broad political institutions and not to their subsidiary administrative units.

The expressed purpose of the governing board in pursuing a legally recognized status was the improvement of educational quality and standards among the black and Puerto Rican schools. The fact that so many new programs of instruction were developed in the district demonstrates that innovation did in fact, though not necessarily in theory, follow decentralization. McCoy's assistant for curriculum, Edwardo Braithwait, reviewing the success of one such program, said: "The average student in this district is three years behind in reading. . . With this program, in six weeks we raised their reading level at least one grade and as much as three grades in some cases." [22] Thus, in the view of the Ocean Hill group, in order to raise the level of education for its black and Puerto Rican children a separate administrative and decision-making unit was needed in the district. As Reverend Oliver observed, under this kind of decentralization the community would "control its own schools and who teaches in them."[23]

Implicit in these demands is a notion of cultural distance between white Americans and blacks and Puerto Ricans. If they had simply wanted to overcome prejudice and discrimination, administrative decentralization should have been sufficient. Moreover, community separation in a city whose policies are primarily, rather than secondarily, racist would not have meant control but rather isolation from resources and "benign neglect," elsewhere known as apartheid. Instead, they sought community control as a means of realizing a cultural identity through educational policy.

Shanker's reply to the Ocean Hill claim of instructional innovation, illustrates the divergent perspective. He maintained, "Decentralization is educationally irrelevant." He added that the problem had to be solved by more money, smaller classes, "more effective" training for teachers, and other administrative procedures. One can only distinguish control over methods of training teachers, for example, from decentralization if one does not mean by that term community control.

108

When Shanker did refer to the Ocean Hill viewpoint, as he seemed to have done on several occasions, he was diametrically opposed. In these instances the teacher's security was frequently mentioned. Yet, it is important to note that the union alluded to a threat to teacher security in a situation where it did not recognize the authority of the precariously decentralized unit. Thus, the fear of community control may have been related to job security but the union attack was upon community control itself. It did not, for example, suggest or consider the possibility of negotiating a contract with the Ocean Hill governing board, which had legal status. More to the point, in separating teacher performance from decentralization, Shanker indicated a belief that teacher status would not have to be threatened by the Ocean Hill governing board. Still, he insisted on numerous occasions during the strikes that "McCoy and the governing board must be removed."[24]

It would be misleading to apply the term due process to what must be identified as concern over the distribution of power, and a desire to secure the union's power position. David Rogers, in his analysis of the City's educational system, depicts the relationship between teacher supervision and the union's power when he argues, "no adequate procedure exists to remove, retrain, or supervise more closely incompetent teachers. The union is more powerful than the ghetto parents."[25] We must distinguish this kind of political interest on the part of the union from job security, which refers specifically to due process in employment.

Observing that the union was one of the groups in a white "power structure" which had excluded racial minorities, Rogers in the early '60s concludes: "The Negroes and Puerto Ricans want much more power, but they can only get it by taking some away from PAT [Parents and Taxpayers Associated] , the moderates, the white liberals, the U. F. T. and the board. This is what the struggle over decentralization really means and it is why the white groups have been so reluctant to endorse the ghetto leadership's demands for community participation in the schools."[26]

In the later years of the decade the struggle remained essentially unchanged though it was considerably exacerbated by the teacher strikes. There is no reason to believe that the earlier prominence of race as a factor in determining lines of division has in any way declined. Notably, in this respect, black teachers did not support the U. F. T. Nevertheless, this chapter has attempted first to distinguish the attitudes pertinent to the school crisis from those which have so broad an impact in American society.[27]

We have discovered that the term decentralization evoked differing cognitive referents for the U. F. T. and the Ocean Hill group when they expressed similar feelings about it. When they perceived decentralization in the same way, meaning community control, their attitudes were in direct opposition. The power of the Union seems to be the specific concern behind U. F. T. opposition. In any case, when the Union entered what Shanker called the "battlefield" of urban schools, it attacked that concept of power the administrators, the governing board, and parents had sought to make a reality in Ocean Hill-Brownsville. The destruction of the small districts which appears to have taken place through subsequent action in the state legislature[28] (where the U. F. T. began its fight) marks another crippling of community control.

The failure of the City and teachers and the Ocean Hill-Brownsville group to find and stick to common conceptual ground in the community control conflict is in the long run inseparable from the divergence in their concepts of the "community." In the short run the conflict appeared as a simple power dispute, which it was to a considerable degree. At that stage, the City and the Mayor were sympathetic with the community. This is perhaps because city officials would have preferred a weaker teacher's union, a preference which might well have been founded in a sincere desire to understand and appease the racial minority. Ultimately, however, the City followed Commissioner Allen in failing to recognize that the Ocean Hill group saw their community, at least for a time, as having a unique cultural identity that was particularly relevant to the educational process. No doubt U. F. T. supporters suspected this self-concept and consequently feared that a white union and unsympathetic teachers would be rejected as cultural non-conformists.

Yet such fears were not justified in the long run, in part because the sense of cultural independence was too nebulous and so lacking in concrete imperatives that it had only a tenuous hold on the district's decision-making. More important, it would be possible for whites to fit in (acculturate) rather than sacrifice their jobs, as had been done during the riots following Martin Luther King's death. On the other hand, the prevailing ideal of the educational process as racially neutral was threatened more deeply than it ever was in simple integration and equal treatment conflicts. Consequently, teachers, black or white, who infuse their work with the ideal of racial neutrality were likely to come under pressure to change.

When the Ford Foundation plan for the experimental school districts was accepted by the City, the lines of authority were not clearly established. Perhaps it was thought that the solution to minority problems in education should come from within the minority communities. Yet as the hasty retrenchment to the traditional distribution of authority shows, it was also believed that

the substance and administration of education should be uniform
except for those changes in the course of work acceptable to everyone who had previously shared in education. All that remained
to insure the survival of this uni-cultural tradition was to consign decentralized districts to the status of lower-echelon administrative units, and this was nearly completed when the District
was denied a voice in the arbitration of its own status. Ironically,
had the U. F. T. conceded to the District leadership its cultural
motives and attendant policy, the District Board might have lost its
apparently tenuous hold on the community.

Latent Differences on "Race"

From the beginning, the Ocean Hill-Brownsville experiment
was an innocent mistake. Everyone involved agrees that its consequences were far from expected. No one expected the Governing
Board to make the strong demands that it did, nor was anyone pre-
pared to see the U. F. T. tenaciously oppose the Board on almost
every point. The U. F. T. realized very early that community
control threatened to "get out of control," particularly because
any redefinition could threaten its functional "island of power"
within the educational system. By the same token, Mayor Lindsay
and the Bundy planning commission may have also forseen the possibility for some shifting in the balance of functional administrative
power as a result of community control. In the case of city officials, however, the failure to forstall such an eventuality could
only be considered a mistake in the light of the union's damaging
reaction. The eventuality which they might well have forstalled,
had they forseen it, was the Governing Board's redefinition of
"community" in terms of race and its reanalysis of education in
terms of culture.

The Ocean Hill-Brownsville group can best be understood as
having had a latent orientation toward race and culture which
inevitably presaged a conflict with the traditional educational
leadership--a leadership which, for its part, maintained the dominant physiological orientation toward race and a compatible bureaucratic orientation toward education. The two orientations predis-
posed, but did not necessitate, a conflict among the actors. In
the prevailing U. F. T. view race was irrelevant to educational
administration, and racism, if present in the conflict, was an
unnecessary additive to a conflict over educational goals and
professional rights. In the developing perspective of the Governing
Board, racial consequences were tied to educational values, and
racism was immanent in any behavior, administrative or otherwise,
which denied the interplay of educational values and cultural background.

111

The essential difference of orientation between the two groups can be traced to the cognitive dimension of race as cultural versus race as physiological. Logically, the U. F. T. could not concede that a physiological factor like race could be inextricably inter- twined with a cultural phenomenon like education; while the Ocean Hill-Brownsville group, with its developing cultural concept of race, came to see the two as inseparable.

The mistake of the planning commission and Mayor's office does not rest in their inability to predict the divergence of orientations which followed their action because the cultural orientation only surfaced after the community control experiment had been launched (and even then it was never consciously articu- lated). Their mistake was first in their failure to recognize that the imposition of a unique subunit of administration on an established and previously independent administration required that members of the new subunit seek their own basis of legiti- macy. The prevailing notion of administrative legitimacy in education, as in most bureaucratic systems, placed a high priority on value-neutrality and on the universality of professionalism (rationalization).[29] In other words, the educational system was presumed to be staffed by experts who could be, if they were not in fact, above the quagmire of ethical and ethnic hostilities and professionally shielded common social biases. Any new administra- tion which questioned these qualities, neutrality and universality, even if only implicitly, had to be rejected. The mere suggestion then that community, ethnic or racial-group values be superimposed on education should be expected to lead to a hostile rejection by established administrators and teachers.[30]

Secondly, the efforts of the Governing Board to ground and expand its new authority on the broadest possible basis should have come as no surprise. Unfortunately, City administrators were also taken in by the neutrality-universality bureaucratic ethic, and they could not therefore envision a substantially different perspective on education. As such, they could not see how the community, however it might choose to define itself, could affect the basic structure of the City's educational system. Per- haps all they wanted to do was to change this structure at the margins—that is, administratively. What they overlooked in giving an unstructured initiative to a previously non-legitimate group was the obligation of that group to react against those authority structures and values which had previously deprived them of legi- timacy.

Consequently, the authorization of community control in a relatively racially homogeneous community was a tacit directive to redefine education in terms of that homogeneity. The minimal

112

logical step then for community leaders was to assert the <u>uniqueness</u> of its educational clientele. Accordingly, Rhody McCoy initiated new instructional programs including paraprofessionalism and black English instruction, as indicated earlier. In all probability, these programs were theoretically possible in the standard educational system. In fact, similar ones have subsequently been tried in other parts of the system. However, non-community control experiments with such innovations can usually be distinguished from community control experiments on two grounds.

First, traditional systems tend to "blame" the student clientele for the inefficacies of traditional education, rather than to thoroughly critique existing professional-educational standards. Thus, the innovations that make their way into the system are frequently labelled as special programs for the disadvantaged. Secondly, community developed innovations are more likely to incorporate a change in long-range educational goals, e.g. achieving a bilingual community through bilingual education, while in the prevailing system changes like bilingual education are only conceived as short-term means for attaining pre-established goals. For example, bilingualism and black English are emphasized in the very early years of schooling as a means of assimilating or adapting children to standard English. An alternative would be <u>accomodating</u> language instruction to variable social goals.[31]

Since the Governing Board could not have fallen easily into the professional ethic of educational administrators and U. F. T. teachers, it should not have been expected to readily defer to "due process" in employment. Due process in the 1968 New York City context meant that a teacher could only be removed for failing to fulfill his professional responsibilities, as those same professionals defined them. Unfortunately for the Governing Board, these responsibilities at least implicitly prescribed good behavior in terms of value-neutrality and universality--two qualities which in their full extension militate against culturally-defined community action.

APPENDIX

Dictionary: Operational Indicators

Decentralization	I	Jobs
	I	
	I	
bureaucrats	I	adequate teacher training
+central+ (e.g. decentralization)	I	contract
community	I	due process
control	I	jobs, employment
district	I	professional standards, practice
force	I	salary, pay
local (power, control)	I	transfer, fire
neighborhood (control)	I	teacher preparation
political structure, system	I	teacher's responsibility
racial conflict, hostility	I	teacher's rights
selling out	I	union responsibility
	I	
	I	
	I	
	I	

Also various prefixes and suffixes on word stems.

U. F. T., References

No.	11	I	No.	4
Per cent	73	I	Per cent	27

Ocean Hill-Brownsville References

No.	13	I	No.	0
Per cent	100	I	Per cent	0

114

1 The "dictionary" consists of phrases and "representative" words rather than single, inclusive word lists.

2 David Rogers, 110 Livingston Street, (New York: Random House, 1968), p. 193.

3 Martin Mayer, The Teachers Strike New York, 1968, (New York, Evanston and London: Harper and Row, Publishers, 1969), pp. 21, 22.

4 Jason Epstein, "The Real McCoy," New York Review of Books, March 13, 1969.

5 Mayer, Op. cit. p. 35.

6 See statement of Fred Nauman (one of the nineteen teachers) issued by the U. F. T.

7 Mayer, Op. cit. pp. 48 and 49.

8 New York Review of Books, Epstein article. Op. cit.

9 See also I. F. Stone's Weekly, November 4, 1968, Vol. XVI, No.22.

10 Mayer, Op. cit. p. 63.

11 Ibid. pp. 74, 75.

12 Ibid. p. 89.

13 Gabriel Almond and Sidney Verba, The Civic Culture (Boston and Toronto: Little, Brown and Company, 1965), p. 14.

14 I believe that these definitions reflect distinctions made by Professor Theodore Lowi.

15 Talcott Parsons, Max Weber: The Theory of Social and Economic Organization, (New York: Oxford University Press, 1947, 1966), pp. 126-127.

16 Philip J. Stone et. al., The General Inquirer. A Computer Approach to Content Analysis, (Cambridge, Massachusetts and London, England: The M.I.T. Press, 1966). See p. 35 on image and theme.

[17] This procedure is meant to elucidate the way in which the present argument has been developed and not to validate it systematically. The appendix contains a list of words and phrases used as indicators of the objects, decentralization and jobs. This list makes up the operational dictionary. See Stone et. al., p. 97, on word count procedures.

[18] New York Times, "Annual Education Review," (Jan. 9, 1969). pp. 67 and 76.

[19] Theodore J. Lowi, At the Pleasure of the Mayor (London: The Free Press of Glencoe, 1964), p. 218. See also Sayre and Kaufman, Governing New York City, 1960.

[20] New York Times, January 9, 1969, pp. 67 and 76.

[21] Ibid., pp. 67 and 76.

[22] New York Times, September 9, 1968.

[23] Ibid., September 13, 1968.

[24] Ibid., September 13, 1968, p. 1 and October 24, 1968, p. 1.

[25] Rogers, Op. cit., p. 480.

[26] Ibid., p. 206. Underlining is my own.

[27] See, for example: Alphonso Pinkney, Black Americans, (Englewood Cliffs, New Jersey: Prentice Hall, Inc., 1969).

[28] Saturday Review, November 16, 1968.

[29] See Robert Dreeben, "The Contribution of Schooling to the Learning of Norms," ed. Sam Sieber and David Wilder. The School in Society, (New York: The Free Press, 1973). He defines universalism in the classroom as the obligation to categorize and relate to people in terms of an abstract organizational or social role model (pp. 72-74). Marilyn Gittell in "Professionalism and Public Participation," eds. Gittell and Hevesi, The Politics of Urban Education, (New York: Praeger, 1969), argues that "education in New York City has become amazingly insulated from public controls. One could describe the situation as an abandonment of public education by key forces of potential power within the city. Bureaucratization and professionalization are contributing factors." p. 156.

[30]See Gerald Moeller, "Bureaucracy and Teachers' Sense of Power," eds. Sieber and Wilder, The School in Society. He finds that bureaucratization reinforces a teacher's sense of power and s security. The larger the bureaucracy, the greater this reinforcement. p. 204.

[31]Remi Clignet, Liberty and Equality in the Educational Process: A Comparative Sociology of Education, (New York: John Wiley and Sons, 1974). He argues: "In the urban context, assimilation-based (teaching) strategy is likely to be maximal in the schools of slums... An assimilation-based teaching tends to prevail because parents and children have not enough resources to challenge the existing system." p. 277.

BIBLIOGRAPHY

Almond, Gabriel andSidney Verba. The Civic Culture. Boston
and Toronto: Little, Brown and Company, 1965.

Clignet, Remi. Liberty and Equality in the Educational Process:
A Comparative Sociology of Education. New York: John
Wiley & Sons, 1974.

Gittell, Marilyn and Alan G. Hevesi, eds. The Politics of Urban
Education. New York: Praeger Publishers, 1969.

Lowi, Theodore J. At the Pleasure of the Mayor. London: The
Free Press of Glencoe, 1964.

Mayer, Martin. The Teachers Strike New York, 1968. New York,
Evanston, and London: Harper and Row, Publishers, 1969.

Parsons, Talcott. Max Weber: The Theory of Social and Economic
Organization. New York: Oxford University Press, 1947, 1966.

Pinkney, Alphonso. Black Americans. Englewood Cliffs, New Jersey:
Prentice Hall, Inc., 1969.

Rogers, David. 110 Livingston Street. New York: Random House,
1968.

Stone, Chuck. Black Political Power in America. Indianapolis,
New York: Dell Publishing Company, Inc., 1970.

Stone, Philip J., et. al. The General Inquirer. A Computer
Approach to Content Analysis. Cambridge, Massachusetts,
and London, England: The M.I.T. Press, 1966.

Journal and Newspaper Articles

Robert Dreeben, "The Contribution of Schooling to the Learning
of Norms," eds. Sam Sieber and David Wilder. The School
in Society. New York: The free Press, 1973.

I. F. Stone's Weekly, Vol. XVI, No. 22, November 4, 1968.

New York Times, May 1968 through January 1969. Selections on
Education.

Epstein, Jason. "The Real McCoy," New York Review of Books,
March 13, 1969.

Gerald Moeller, "Bureaucracy and Teachers' Sense of Power,"
eds. Sam Sieber and David Wilder. <u>The School in Society</u>,
New York: The Free Press, 1973.

Roberts, Wallace. "The Battle for Urban Schools," <u>Saturday
Review</u>, November 16, 1968.

CHAPTER V

Ideology and Policy As an Unstable Dialectic:
Nationalism on Newly Integrated Campuses

When the British held India during the nineteenth century,
a question arose over the kind of education the Indian elite should
receive. Some Englishmen argued for a ressurection of traditional
Indian education, the study of classical Indian history, Indian
literature, and Indian institutions. Other Englishmen believed that
the only real education was one based in Western civilization,
especially at Oxford. The latter faction, lead by Lord Macaulay
won the debate. Even the revolutionary colonial elite (Gandhi,
Nkrumah, Kenyatta), trained by Western intellectuals, found it
difficult not to assimilate Western standards of success and excel-
lence as their own.[1]

How much more difficult then was it for a people who were
commonly regarded as having no past, no tradition, no literature,
to educate themselves--to educate themselves, that is, so they
could find and know themselves. It must have seemed ironic to
those black students in American universities in the 1960's that
"true" liberation from slavery had post-dated the Emancipation
Proclamation by one hundred years; that external official liberation had not brought about internal liberation; that when the
black man had fought and agitated for his freedom, he had fought
merely for the values of his master's world, had fought for white
freedom and white justice. But what were his values and where
was the self for which he might have fought?

The answer to this question assumes two dimensions for our
purposes. The first dimension involves the cognitive awareness
of the black student in regard to his race and the mediating in-
fluences that lead him to attach values to that race. The second
dimension involves white America, both in terms of individuals and
institutions, and their relationship to the black student. We
must consider, first of all, the relationship between growing.
numbers of black students and the movement for black studies.

120

Black Students: Then and Now

The black studies movement of recent years has brought about the most intense intra-black debate since the controversy that pitted Booker T. Washington against W.E.B. DuBois. This debate is exacerbated by the increasing number of students coming to campus from lower-class ghettoes. The number of Negro college students has grown from 15,000 largely middle-class youth in 1927 to 814,000 in 1972. Thus, says Raymond Wolters in his important work on black college rebellions of the 1920's, cultural alienation is the trait that most distinguishes contemporary cultural nation-alists from the black college rebels of the 1920's[2] While the earlier black rebels were not accommodationists, they steered clear of Garvey and the separatist nationalism of their day. Their aim was to be included in the prevailing culture, and they worked assiduously to raise the academic standards of their colleges to the level of their white counterparts.

Among the black college student rebellions of the 1920's, only that at Howard University takes on a decidedly racial orien-tation.[3] Two factors may have played a role in determining the character of the Howard conflict. In the first place, federal assistance to Howard freed it from financial dependence on church boards and organized philanthropy. Thus Howard's black students did not come under the tutelary discipline that prevailed at other leading black schools like Fisk, and extracurricular activities similiar to those enjoyed by most white students were open to them.[4] One might assume that this limited freedom bred the desire for complete freedom as their relative deprivation was made clearer. The second unique contributing factor in the Howard case was the university's location. Being the only black university in a large Negro community, Howard attracted many lower-class students who could not afford room and board at more remote residential colleges.[5] While there is no direct evidence that either of these factors played a particularly significant role in the attempt to oust J. Stanley Durkee as Howard's President, they were unique among the black colleges at that time and more importantly they emerge as general factors in the black rebellions of the sixties.

Perhaps Howard's black faculty deserves more credit than its students for contributing to the racial character of the conflict. Professors like Alain Locke, Carter G. Woodson, Kelly Miller, and William Leo Hansberry were attempting to supplement the university's curriculum with courses and projects that would legitimize the sense of group identification as early as 1901. Yet for the next twenty years the university found it difficult to recognize the academic legitimacy of black studies and gave such efforts little support. The absence of support led these faculty members to note, in the words of Locke, that the race was losing its "finest social products," as able black students succumbed to the "prevalent materialistic individualism of middle-class American life." He concluded that "if there is anything . . . particularly needed in Negro education it is the motive and ideal of group service."[6]

Although Locke and his colleagues were laying the foundation for cultural pluralism rather than separation, their arguments ran counter to those that dominated the era. During the first half of the Twentieth Century white educational policy has promoted disciplinary education while black educational policy focused on practical education. Booker T. Washington at Tuskegee, A. A. Turner at Florida A & M, James Gregg at Hampton, and other educational policy-makers downplayed or soft-pedaled cultural education. It should be noted that their notion of a cultural education was not one that included black studies but rather a traditional liberal arts education that might lead to "social equality." Schools like Fisk that moved too far in this direction were put into reverse gear by those in tune with the secular foundations and educational boards that controlled college endowments. One example will serve to make the point: Under Fayette McKenzie at Fisk the student government was disbanded and dissent forbidden. The Fisk Herald, the oldest student publication among black colleges, was suspended and the alumni journal wrote only of the things the white south wanted to hear. The Administration rejected a request for recognition of a campus chapter of the NAACP, and the university librarian was instructed to inspect NAACP literature and excise articles deemed too radical. Male-female student interaction was strictly forbidden and this policy was justified with repeated assertions that black adolescents were particularly sensuous beings who would abandon themselves to indulgence if they were not subjected to firm control.[7] At schools like Fisk and Tuskegee blacks were to acquire the "internal social structure" and skills that would make them desirable to white industry.[8] Consequently, the two elements of black higher education in the early Twentieth Century were a vocational curriculum combined with twenty four hour morality training.

The success of DuBois and the Fisk alumni, along with the students, in removing President McKenzie despite his successful endowment drive may be attributed to the unusual student solidarity and the successful public relations work of DuBois. They were greatly aided by the President's decision to call on white Nashville policemen to aid in restoring order after a student disturbance. This decision infuriated blacks both inside and outside the college community and speeded McKenzie's removal. Yet DuBois was one of the few to see the large implications of the

Fisk protest. While most students in 1924 and 1925 confined their
focus to disciplinary rules and campus organizations (they did
not insist on a black successor to McKenzie), DuBois saw it as
"more than opposition to a program of education. It was opposition to a system and that system was part of the economic development of the United States at that time."[9]

DuBois was able to go beyond the argument that the races
were at different stages of cultural evolution which necessitated
a different level of educational curriculum. The argument was not
only culturally but economically motivated. Black higher education not only raised the spector of social equality but also
ruined good fieldhands.

From Individual to Institutional Racism

Given the historic conservatism of black colleges controlled
by white boards of trustees or more recently conservative black
boards of trustees and a tradition of piety that remained in force
long after the leading white colleges had deemphasized their concern for moral uplift and had begun to stress secular scholarship,
it is not unusual that growing numbers of black students began to
enroll in white institutions as barriers to their admission began
to crumble. Lacking a sense of community found in black colleges
and concerned about the relevance of their education for blacks
as a group, they began to question not only the content of their
instruction but also the very structure of the university. They
entered a situation in which it was readily apparent (more so
than at poverty-stricken, grantless black schools) that the vast
resources of the university were used to protect the status quo.
Theodore Lowi credits students in general for seeing and articulating this political role:

> services in the contemporary university are
> essentially policies that involve collective
> choices, that collective choices involve advan-
> tages and disadvantages in the struggle for
> rewards that society has to offer, and that
> such struggles involve power, which is the
> very opposite of the ideal of education.[10]

Thus, the students, both black and white, did not politicize the
university--they found it in that state. Moreover, the university as an institution was involved in policy that was essentially
contradictory to its stated goals.

The precarious political position of the university was
intensified by its cultural role. As the keeper of American

culture it is inherently conservative yet it must give the public
appearance of encouraging or at least tolerating dissenting views
(unlike historic black colleges). Once challenged with institutional racism, both in its curriculum and its power distribution,
it is unwilling to admit bias but forced to tolerate dissent.
In this permissive atmosphere the tactics of the civil rights
movement (which was supported by the liberal college community)
were used by black students for a purpose with which many formerly supportive faculty and students could not agree--the granting
of power to a group of students whose aspirations and sense of
education were alien to the entire white academic community.[11]

Universities in the United States, at least those outside
the South, have traditionally prided themselves on the absence
of racism in the academic community. Education has long been
regarded as the way to self-enlightenment and the broadening of
horizons. The secular philanthropists of the early Twentieth
Century often regarded white education as more beneficial to the
Negro race than black education: "the education 'of one untaught
white man to the point that knowledge and not prejudice will
guide his conduct. . . is worth more to the black man himself than
the education of ten Negroes.'"[12] More recently, colleges had
moved to eliminate obvious signs of racism in housing, dining,
athletics and admissions. The Negro was to receive the same treatment as any other student.

It came as a great surprise then, when the black students
in the sixties charged this great liberal institution with racism.
Administrators and faculty reacted with genuine bewilderment when
they were singeled out not for individual acts of discrimination
but rather for "institutional racism." Were not the same admission standards applied to black and white alike with no reference
to race on admission forms? Of course the reply was that viewing
race neutrally was irrelevant. Racism was not merely a question
of individual perceptions or attitudes but was institutionalized.
It was not only physical but also cultural. The question was not
the administration of the standards but rather the standards themselves. They were designed to test the knowledge of white middle-
class culture and not the black experience. To view race neutrally
in such circumstances was to deny the identity of the black student and to predetermine his failure.

The Black Studies Movement

Although those black students who engaged in some of the
first demonstrations concerning black studies may have owed some
of their inspiration to the white radicals of the "free speech"
movement, they generally regarded black studies as "their thing."
In fact, the most important New Left activity in northern

California prior to the autumn of 1964 involved civil rights.
Mario Savio, having returned from a stint in the South for SNCC,
argued that "the same rights are at stake in both places [Berkeley
and Mississippi]--the right to participate as citizens in a
democratic society."13 The difference was that white students
were not concerned with their own victimization while black students realized that they could not gain a knowledge of themselves
by following white radicals. In the words of DuBois, the black
race needed its own leaders.

Despite the wide range of universities experiencing dis-
ruptions, the demands were surprisingly similar:

1) Official recognition of the local organization of black students as a valid campus
   organization (which usually meant access to
   a share of the Student Activities Funds and
   other amenities);

2) the introduction of a black studies curriculum;

3) substantial increases in the black student
   enrollment, black faculty, and black coun-
   selors;

4) the provision of a "cultural" center or
   meeting place for black students;

5) the elimination of "institutional racism"

Some observers of the black studies movement have viewed these
demands as an extension of the community control struggle in public
school education.14

Black studies curricula in general have necessitated that
the courses be taught by blacks and that they relate to the local
black community. In one sense these demands parallel the demands
for community control over public schools. Yet only one step
removed from this perspective are the views of Theodore Draper
who sees black studies as a form of black nationalism:

Black quasi-nationalism in America, however,
has been forced to look for a surrogate sovereignty, a substitute for a nation. This need
is the unfulfilled and unfulfillable wish behind
the demands for separate, autonomous Black or
Afro-American Studies in our colleges and uni-
versities.15

Draper argues that such sovereignty is a subsidized sovereignty. Moreover, he says, one must distinguish between the case for Black Studies and the case for Black Schools of Black Studies.

While one may or may not agree with Draper, it is true that the issue of Black Studies has illustrated the gap between the supporters of traditional "Negro colleges" and the promoters of "Black Studies." James Turner, director of Cornell's Black Studies program, held that the demand for Black Studies now and a Black University to come was "opposed to the traditional Negro colleges which reflect the curriculum of white institutions."[16]

As stated earlier, Negro colleges have historically been placed in the role of playing catch-up to white colleges. These colleges have had neither the resources nor, in most cases, the freedom to offer non-traditional programs of study. The foremost proponents of black studies have resided on white campuses-- with a few exceptions like Dr. Vincent Harding who operated from the newly created Institute of the Black World. Some would argue that the best black brains have been "bought up" by the white institutions. Others would argue that the traditionally "Negro colleges" drove their most creative thinkers away as a result of their conservatism. In any case, the fact remains that the "Black Studies" movement was confined primarily to white campuses. Perhaps we can begin to understand this phenomenon by looking at several case histories.

San Francisco State College was the first school to intro- duce a Black Studies program. In the spring of 1966 it offered a course in Black Nationalism that was followed in the academic year of 1967-68 with a Black Studies Curriculum consisting of eleven courses. However, this growth had taken place in a situa- tion so inflamed that the President decided to appoint a Black Studies Coordinator who had been chosen by the Black Students' Union. The appointment of Dr. Nathan Hare, a black sociologist who had been too radical[17] for Howard University, was made with- out consulting or even informing the Vice-President for Academic Affairs, the Council of Academic Deans, or the faculty. By the end of 1968 the Black Students' Union was demanding an autonomous program with the sole power to hire faculty and grant degrees.[18]

Hare set about building a Black Studies program that was "revolutionary" and "nationalistic." He saw field work or commu- nity involvement as the central focus for a Department of Black Studies. To bring about this development Hare believed it nec- essary

> to inspire and sustain a sense of collective
> destiny as a people and a consciousness of the

126

value of education in a technological society.
A cultural base, acting as a leverage for other
aspects of Black ego development and academic
unit, must accordingly be spawned and secured.[19]

Hare claimed, and there is some evidence to support his contention,
that black students do respond directly and positively to a black
instructor. Opponents of an all-black faculty would argue that
such a department must include white students and therefore under-
cut the black instructor argument. The controversial Dr. Hare
was subsequently dismissed by the equally controversial new
President Dr. S. I. Hayakawa.

The pioneering effort in Black Studies at San Francisco State
leaves us with a number of implications that would be repeated.
In the first place, it appears that the selection of Dr. Hare by
the President was as much a political decision as an educational
one. The President had by-passed the traditional appointment route
to grant black student demands. Thus it appears that the Black
Student's Union was successful in changing traditional university
policy. Secondly, Hare's whole concept of a Department of Black
Studies is radically different from the traditional concept of
that academic unit. The Department of Black Studies is seen as
a cultural base which serves the needs of the black student ego
and the black community. Finally, the emphasis on collective
rather than individual stimulation is antithetical to the whole
notion of severe individual competition in the American college
and presupposes a common base (race) that can be stimulated.

Hare sought to establish a black community within the university that was capable of doing things outside of the prevailing
norms. Of course, such behavior when viewed from the traditional
perspective appears deviant--just as does most black political
activity. In other words, black studies can only be justified as
opposed to, or perhaps indifferent toward, established educational
policy because it seeks to adapt the policy to the students and
their milieu and not vice-versa. Sociologist Hare began by per-
suading San Francisco State to waive the entrance exam for 250
extra black students with expectations of more exemptions in the
future. These students were "to be used--not to be exploited,
because they will gain something in return--manpower to help bring
about the sort of aggressiveness and pro-blackness of the students
at the lower levels in the school system of the black community."[20]
These students were being used to build a socio-psychologically
receptive community for black students on white campuses. The
result, says Hare, is better all-around academic performance:

127

About forty-five students in our Black Students'
Union (who fathered the idea of the black studies
curriculum) were on probation before we began
the black studies program. Of the forty-five
students who were on probation when the courses
were instituted last semester, only twenty-three
remained by the end of the semester. We also
discovered that it wasn't just a case of their
getting good grades in their black courses; they
also were doing better in their white courses,
in almost every case, because, having acquired
the new sense of pride and involvement in the
education process they wanted to convey that in
their classes. [21]

Hare would like to see this new sense of pride and achievement
developed in the black community outside the university so that
the black child might benefit from it before he reaches the
college level.

Antioch College, in Yellow Springs, Ohio, long an innovator
in higher education, was to take the concept of Black Studies one
step further. Black students at Antioch succeeded in creating
what had only been implied at San Francisco State, an Afro-
American Studies Institute which excluded white students and
faculty. An editorial in the Antioch Review states that "several
hundred Antioch students and a substantial number of faculty had
earlier petitioned the college to permit "academic self-determination for Black students."[22] These students received $10,000
in August of 1968. The editorial goes on to state that many of
these students would not normally have qualified for Antioch's
regular academic program:

Many of the Black students who established the
Afro-American Studies Institute (AASI) had
originally entered Antioch as Negroes under the
auspices of the Rockfeller Interracial Program,
which was designed to bring to the College "disadvantaged" students who would otherwise have
not been considered likely prospects for a liberal
arts education. [23]

Thus the AASI provided an "alternative" to Antioch's regular
curriculum.

The teachers in the AASI program were all black Ph.D candidates at the University of Chicago. During the year 1969 these
graduate "consultants" would visit Antioch once a month for three
days of classes, lecturing ten hours a day. A student spokesman

for the program insisted that the inclusion of whites would
"inhibit fundamental emotions from being expressed." In a reaction
to the program's exclusionary policy and academic stature, black
psychologist Kenneth B. Clark resigned from the Antioch College
Board of Trustees. Clark protested that

> a university could not surrender to student control
> a Black Studies Institute with exclusionary charac-
> teristics and without even minimal academic standards
> if it truly valued the humanity of blacks. If the
> university does not insist that Negroes be as
> rigorously trained as whites to compete in the
> area of real power, or that studies of racism be as
> thoroughly and systematically pursued as studies of
> nuclear physics, one might question whether it is
> really serious.24

Clark stated that the AASI program was only a "charade of power"
and that a Black Studies program must also include the education
of whites as one of its goals.

In a companion Antioch Review article Stephen Lythcott defends
Antioch's Black Studies program. He thinks that it is more important to reorient black students, create a new value system and
help the black community than it is to educate Antioch whites.
Lythcott's views closely parallel those of Hare in their emphasis
on supporting the black ego and on service to the black community.
However, Antioch blacks were able to go one step further and exclude
whites from their program.

Clark, unlike another prominent black opponent of Black Studies,
Martin Kilson, does believe that there is some intellectual
validity in studying the black experience. He is concerned, however, that the program be as academically rigorous as that of any
department and that the Black Studies program be open to white
students. Blacks have only been given enough power to hurt themselves.

The case of Black Studies at Cornell University represents
the extreme in black student support for academic autonomy in
that a number of black students were willing to die for it. In
the fall of 1968 Cornell instituted an Afro-American Studies
Prog.am, financed by a one million dollar trustee grant and
supervised by a committee composed of nine white faculty members
and administrators and eight black students. By December of 1968
militant members of the Afro-American Society had challenged the
structure and plans of the committee. In a statement to President
Perkins the Afro-American Society defined their position in regard

129

to Black Studies. "The validity of a program is determined by those who have the power to define and to set its limits and goals," said the students. Blacks must have this power and whites could only contribute in "an advisory, nondecision making or financial capacity." The Afro-American Society proposed a program of "independent status" but based on financial aid through grants by the university, private foundations and endowments. Thus the objective of this nonnegotiable demand was "the creation of a Black College of Black students and scholars within a white university which will deal with the problems of Black America."[25]

While the administration and faculty refused to go along with the demand for an independent black college, President Perkins did begin to deal with the Afro-American Society as if it were the recognized bargaining agency of all the black students. In May, James E. Turner, a graduate student at Northwestern, was selected as Director of the Center for Afro-American Studies although no one knew what the Center was supposed to do or what the new Director's plans were. It later developed that Mr. Turner hoped to create "an international center for Black Studies" at Cornell. The ultimate aim was to prepare "a new cadre of intellectuals" and "a new kind of professional school" including technology and science as well as black history and culture. A "home center" would be based at Cornell with an "Urban Resident Center" located in a black community. The first two years of a students' college career would be spent on academic work at the Cornell Center. The third year would be spent at the urban center and the final year writing a thesis on the previous year's experience. While Turner did not reject white students outright he pointed out that few would be qualified to participate in the Center's program:

> While seriously considering such factors as
> academic training and standing, we must place
> the greatest relevance to the Black community
> and his commitment to work towards the solution
> of its problems. We have neither the time or
> resources to operate a race relations project
> wherein well-meaning but inexperienced and
> dysfunctional white students would occupy posi-
> tions that might better be filled by Blacks.
> Of course relevent and equally well-qualified
> (background, experience, commitment) whites are
> welcome, but such qualified candidates will
> undoubtedly be rare.[26]

Turner said that his program was directed toward the "second stream of Black student" that probably would not attend college at all if his program did not exist.

It can be seen that the Cornell program shares an emphasis
on community involvement with the San Francisco State and Antioch
programs. Moreover, all three programs would tend to exclude or
limit white participation. Antioch and Cornell express a particular concern for those students that might not make it in a
traditional college program—either through lack of interest or
ability. However, the distinguishing factor in the growth of
Cornell's Black Studies program is the direct threat of violence.
Whereas, President Hayakawa of San Francisco State later brought
in police forces to restore order to that campus and the President
of Antioch conceded almost entirely to black student demands,
Cornell's President steered a middle-course.

President Perkins did not bring in outside forces yet he
opposed the proposed program's "complete autonomy." The result
was a gradual escalation in the black student's tactics. Tactics
ranged from a December 1968 spree with toy guns to an April 1969
building takeover with real guns. Concessions were made to the
gun-bearing black students in return for evacuation of the building.
When the full faculty failed to ratify the agreement, threats
were made on the lives of a number of faculty and administrators.
The following day the faculty reversed itself and Perkins and a
number of professors resigned. In a speech delivered to summer
school students a month later, AAS leader Tom Jones explained the
events at Cornell:

> 'I'm speaking to you tonight,' he began, 'because
> I expect that possibly if you understand what's
> happening, you might put yourselves in the way
> of stopping it so we can go on about our develop-
> ment as individuals and as a Black nation.' Then
> he told what had inspired him and his followers:
> 'The purpose of our Black Studies program was
> number one, to give us that psychological freedom
> of self-definition, to define what we are now,
> what we have been as a people, and what we will
> be as a people and as a nation in the future.
> The second purpose of the Black Studies program
> was to teach us the political methods, the poli-
> tical ideology to lead to the kind of political
> freedom and economic self-determination that we
> have to have.' For these purposes, he went on,
> they had decided on a number of 'persuasive steps'
> to force the university to have them recognize
> what has to be for our lives, not only here in
> Ithaca and on the campus of Cornell University,
> but as a Black nation.[27]

In Jones' statement one can see that the Cornell program, like those of Antioch and San Francisco State, was aimed at least in part at fulfilling the psychological needs of the black students. The emphasis on a "Black nation" reinforces the goal of self-determination.

Although many black militants praised the power of the gun at Cornell, Kenneth Clark was quick to object. He states that the armed black students at Cornell had no real power and were at the mercy of the white majority. "To the extent that whites encouraged in blacks acceptance of this pretense of power, they are participating in but one more manifestation of an old racism."[28]

Clark would appear to favor the type of Black Studies program developed at Yale. After meeting with black student representatives, President Kingman Brewster appointed a committee consisting of four faculty and four members of the Black Student Alliance at Yale in early 1968. The committee decided to base its Afro-American studies program on an area studies model that conformed to the academic standards at Yale College. A faculty committee composed of members of the various departments and special studies programs administered the new program. The program was open to both black and white students and faculty with teaching personnel required to have appointments in one of the formal disciplines. On December 12, 1968, the Yale College faculty unanimously approved a degree-granting Afro-American studies program with a strong disciplinary emphasis combined with summer field work.[29]

In comparing the Yale experience to those at San Francisco State, Antioch, and Cornell, one sees some important distinctions. Most basically, the difference is one between Black Studies and a Black College of Black Studies. One finds similarities in the emphasis on field work and the black experience. However, it is at the point of administration that the real differences emerge. It is not so much what will be taught as it is who will teach, who will learn, who will grant degrees.

At this point it might be useful to look at the actors involved. It has been shown that many of the students involved in the San Francisco State and Antioch programs were "special students." That is, they would not normally be attracted to schools like San Francisco State and Antioch or they would not normally be qualified to attend these schools or both. Browne points out that some of these "disadvantaged" students are:

> extremely conservative and eager to "make good"
> in an individualistic sense, others of them see
> their educational opportunity as a means not for

132

personal aggrandizement but as a lever to force
the changes in society which will liberate all
blacks from their oppressive bondage.[30]

Thus some of the students involved in the Black Studies movement
approach a university career from a non-traditional viewpoint.
The university is a political instrument to be used in the liberation of other "disadvantaged" black people.

Of course, the other approach that emerges from this discussion of Black Studies is that of black autonomy. If black
students can choose faculty, grant degrees, and exclude whites,
then they can exclude competition and individualism. Formerly
unacceptable black students are now in the position of determining
what is and is not acceptable. It is this "anti-intellectualism"
that Kenneth Clark opposes. He believes that black students pushing
such programs are deluding themselves and that white administrators who aid them are guilty of practicing racism.

Clark's charges involve us in a final area of concern—the
development of Black Studies on white campuses. Surely it must
seem strange to hear James Turner talk about making Cornell
University in Ithaca, New York, the world-wide center of Afro-
American studies. Why not Howard University in Washington, D.C.?

From Private to Public Policy

Even taking into consideration the historic conservatism of
the Negro college campus,[31] true black self-consciousness may
have required the proximity of whites. The black American, who
knew himself to be different from his white counterpart, lacked
the stimuli to declare his own being. The submerged nature of
his twoness, American and black, hindered the development of self-
consciousness and independent values or standards. On white
campuses in the sixties the lines were made clear and the struggle
provided an opportunity to work out externally what had built up
internally in the form of cognitive knowledge. Like Fanon's
colonized, college confrontations provided him with the means of
becoming who he was. Accordingly one of the first black studies
demands was for courses in African languages—the language question
being symptomatic of the problem of assimilation.

The shift in focus from individual to institutional racism is
in fact an attack on white culture. Individual acts of racism
in the university are almost always covert because they are not
truly self-conscious; they are cultural.[32] That whites have a
one-sided cultural concept indicates, as mentioned earlier, that

133

it is a mediated form of seeing race. The earlier cognitive position of white Americans was "genetic." That is, blacks were regarded as biologically different and the white race was irrevocably
superior. Blacks, on the other hand, were willing to admit the
biological differences but attached no social significance to
them. Given the opportunity, blacks could meet white standards.
However, implicit in this view is the notion that blacks lack
the ability to develop their own culture. The various levels
of consciousness surrounding black demands have resulted in confusing, if not contradictory, positions. For example, the Summer
Research Report of the 1969 Cornell Constituent Assembly reflects
the conflict in regard to admissions policy for courses in the
Center for Afro-American Studies:

> Testimony collected by the research group in
> the summer of 1969 offers persuasive evidence
> that in semesters ahead, the University may well
> be faced with a genuine conflict between the
> social and political goal of integration, generally
> expressed by the white liberal community, and the
> educational goal of providing a classroom setting
> in which the black man's experience in American
> can be most meaningfully analyzed and understood
> by Cornell's black students. It is the position
> of our research group that in the presence of
> such conflict, Cornell should choose the edu-
> cational goal rather than the political one,
> this preference being entirely consistent with
> the historic conception of a university.[33]

Yet when Antioch announced plans to pursue the "educational goal"
and establish a black studies institute excluding whites the
Department of Health, Education, and Welfare threatened to cut
off all federal funds going to Antioch.

The tactics used by black students in making their demands
challenged the traditional university community adjudicative
systems. For example, black students at Cornell claimed that the
university could not fairly adjudicate matters pertaining to
black student actions because it was a party to the action. The
Afro-American Society called for some impartial and disinterested
group to mediate the dispute, as in the case of labor-management
conflicts. The Cornell judicial council claimed that the analogy
was false and the judicial boards made their decisions independently and on behalf of the entire university community. In the
Afro-American Society response the black students stated:

> The university is not a classless society as
> the committee (FCSA) pretends and the present
> judiciary committee is the agent of the adminis-
> tration representing ultimately neither students
> in general nor black students in particular.
> As such it has no legitimacy to judge political
> acts directed against the university administra-
> tion.[34]

Black students highlighted the distinction between "political
activity" directed at public issues like burning draft cards and
"political activity" directed at the university itself.

A final question raised by the events at Cornell in particular has to do with the violation of academic freedom. A group
of professors from outside the Cornell community were invited to
examine this issue. They reported that at least eight of the
Government professors they talked to believed academic freedom
had been infringed upon. A great deal of self-censorship was
discovered. At least one professor was hesitating to give a
course on South Africa. Others were carefully editing their notes
lest they invite confrontation. One faculty member stated that
self-censorship

> takes place because we do not have confidence
> that we will not stand alone against those who
> would use coercive means to express their dis-
> agreement. . . I edit my notes on urban politics
> because I lack faith in my colleagues throughout
> the campus. I do so to avoid being accused by
> the Dean of being "ignorant and insensitive."
> There is a widespread feeling that the Adminis-
> tration cannot be trusted to back up a besieged
> faculty member in any future "academic freedom
> incident".[35]

Cornell, then, clearly reveals the friction created by the black
studies movement between administrators and faculty.

Tom Jones, a leader of Cornell's Afro-American Society,
presents us with an alternate view of academic freedom:

> Clearly, academic freedom must mean the freedom
> to pursue one's educational objectives in a
> climate of mutual respect and security. It also
> means that as a member of the institutional society,
> one has a right to express and make known one's
> views on the policies and general state of affairs
> in that society. But academic freedom also means

135

that one has the responsibility not to attempt
to restrict or to prevent others from expressing
and making known their viewpoints on the policies
and general state of affairs in the university
society. We see that nowhere does the term imply
that one segment of the community has a monopoly
on academic freedom to imply that any one segment
or group in the society has the right to totally
control the law-making and governance of the
society--such monopoly of power should be called,
more appropriately, academic power, not freedom.[36]

For at least some of the students, academic freedom must not be
confined to members of the faculty alone. Such a position poses
a dilemma for those that would label the student rebellion as anti-
intellectual. Moreover, the dilemma faced is different for administrators than it is for faculty members. Black students, it
would appear, are more concerned with educational objectives than
racial balancing.

Conclusion

On the international level, no respectable social scientist
would think of analysing French, British, Soviet, or Chinese social
and economic policy without a serious look at their respective
systems of higher education. Key schools with specific curricula
perform a direct and vital function in the maintenance of the
state. Yet the American system of higher education has, until
recently, escaped any responsibility for American society in general. In the words of a black student at Tougaloo College, "if
schools like Brown [Tougaloo's "big brother"] had been truly edu-
cating their students then the state of the country and the world
would be a lot different."[37] Higher education has been viewed
as an absolute good with little attention focused on the type of
education offered, the structure of the university, or the services rendered. Student activism surrounding the war in Vietnam
and black studies must be credited with holding the university,
as a societal institution, accountable for its actions.

The contradiction between the ideal state of education and
the political reality of the university reaches its zenith in an
educational system in which the norm is technocratic.[38] The short-
term problem solving ethic or "service" orientation currently in
vogue cannot escape a political role. If universities have power--
in the form of information--to solve immediate socio-economic
problems, they must represent the social interests of the dominant
regime.[39] Student objections to the "multiversity" as a "component
part of the military-industrial complex" had the effect of poli-

ticizing what were once regarded as private conflicts. Matters
that were once regarded as the business of trustees, administration,
and faculty, were now of public concern. These matters ranged from
academic freedom, university investments, tenure and university-
government contracts to co-ed living, de-emphasis of athletics,
and the use of pot. Jurgen Habermas states that "difficulties
that a mere two or three years ago would have passed for private
matters. . . now claim political significance and ask to be justified in political concepts.[40] The rebellion of students has led
to the rebellion of housewives, assembly-line workers, and homo-
sexuals.

In his Toward A Rational Society, Habermas outlines three
responsibilities of the university beyond that of immediately
technically exploitable knowledge:

> First, the university has the responsibility
> of ensuring that its graduates are equipped, no
> matter how indirectly, with a minimum of quali-
> fications in the area of extra functional abili-
> ties. . . .
>
> Second, it belongs to the task of the university
> to transmit, interpret, and develop the cultural
> tradition of the society. . . .
>
> Third, the university has always fulfilled a
> task that is not easy to define; today we would
> say that it forms the political consciousness of
> its students.[41]

The views of the German philosopher Habermas are remarkably similar to those expressed by DuBois at the turn of the century in the
Souls of Black Folk. At the center of his debate with Booker T.
Washington was the notion that practical education excluded the
development of political consciousness among blacks or more specifically black leadership. Moreover, DuBois saw that proper political consciousness--knowing one's self--must be developed in an
environment of cultural pluralism not cultural assimilation.

In the current struggle over black studies, liberal whites--
whose consciousness has been limited to physical integration--
have ostensibly accepted black cultural pluralism on campus but
really reflect a culturally assimalitionist orientation. Black
students on white campuses also present a puzzling picture. While
many believe that "the predominately Negro colleges, aside from
providing education of a recognizedly inferior quality, suffer
from attitudes imposed on them by the white community and white
dominated boards of trustees,"[42] they are torn between the market-

place and the black community. Access to superior technical resources and exposure to the dominant culture make them highly desirable in the post-college market place. A common attitude is expressed by a Yale junior: "black studies is interesting, but black people can't afford an interesting major. We want Yale to pay off immediately--starting with $20,000 a year."[43]

While the nature of the conflict between black students and those who control educational policy has reached a higher level--private to public and individual to institutional--and shifted its locus from the black campus to the white campus, the danger remains the same. The economic and political reality of the post-college job market forces culture into the background. Yet the outlook for the seventies and eighties is more favorable than that of the twenties and thirties because blacks have reached a necessary stage of cognitive development. They know that they are the equal of their white counterparts not because they meet his standards but because they meet their own standards. Whether separation serves as an end in itself, useful only in the college community, or whether it serves as a tactic to be used in an attempt to change the entire relationship of the university to society in general remains to be seen.

CHAPTER V
FOOTNOTES

[1]Troy Duster in Immanuel Wallerstein and Paul Starr (eds.) The
University Crisis Reader (N.Y.: Random House, 1971) pp. 34--341.

[2]Raymond Wolters, The New Negro on Campus (Princeton, N.J.:
Princeton University Press, 1975) p. 348.

[3]According to Nathan Hare this orientation was reversed in 1966
when Howard's President James Nabrit announced a plan to make
Howard "sixty percent white" by 1970, a plan opposed by the
entire student body. See Hare's "The Battle for Black Studies"
The Black Scholar, May, 1972, p. 35.

[4]Wolters, The New Negro on Campus, p.71.

[5]Ibid., p. 72.

[6]Ibid., p. 89.

[7]Ibid, p. 34. Note that the emphasis on Victorian morality is
heavily emphasized in all black colleges of that era as
evidenced by the extremely high percentage of clergymen--both
black and white--serving as college presidents.

[8]See Martin Carnoy, Education as Cultural Imperialism, (N.Y.:
McKay, 1974) and Bennett Harrison, Education, Training and the
Urban Ghetto (Baltimore: John Hopkins University Press, 1972)
on the role of public schools in the socialization of lower class
children for economic interests.

[9]W.E.B. DuBois, The Autobiography of W.E.B. DuBois (N.Y.:
International Publishers, 1968) p. 241.

[10]Theodore J. Lowi, The Politics of Disorder (N.Y.: Basic Books,
1971) p. 125.

[11]Allen B. Ballard The Education of Black Folk, (N.Y.: Harper,
1973) p. 42.

[12]Wolters, The New Negro on Campus, p. 14.

[13]Mario Savio in Edward J. Bacciocco, The New Left in America
(Stanford, Calif.: Hoover Institution Press, 1974) p. 155.

[14]See Robert Browne, "The Challenge of Black Student Organizations"
Freedomways, Fall, 1968, p. 325.

[15] Theodore Draper, The Rediscovery of Black Nationalism (N.Y: Viking Press) p. 149.

[16] James Turner quoted in Draper p. 158.

[17] See Hare, "The Battle for Black Studies" pp. 38-39.

[18] Theodore Draper, The Rediscovery of Black Nationalism (N.Y.: Viking Press, 1970) p. 149.

[19] Nathan Hare in John Bunzel, "Black Studies at San Francisco State" The Public Interest, p. 32.

[20] Nathan Hare in Armstead Robinson, (ed.) Black Studies in the University (New Haven, Conn.: Yale University Press, 1969) p. 119.

[21] Ibid., p. 113.

[22] "Editorial" Antioch Review, Summer, 1969, p. 43.

[23] Ibid., pp. 143-144.

[24] Ibid., p. 147.

[25] Draper, The Rediscovery of Black Nationalism, p. 152.

[26] James Turner in Ibid., p. 160.

[27] Draper, p. 156.

[28] Kenneth Clark in, Ibid., p. 157.

[29] Draper, pp. 162-163.

[30] Browne, "The Challenge of Black Student Organizations" p. 327.

[31] See David Riesman and Christopher Jeneks, "The American Negro College" Harvard Educational Review (Volume 37, 1967) and Winfred Godwin, "The Black College as System" Daedalus Summer, 1971, on the character of Negro Colleges.

[32] Institutional racism could allow university officials to deny separate housing to blacks stating that interracial living units promoted social education while permitting exclusive white fraternities and sororities. See Wallerstein and Starr, The University Crisis Reader, p. 305.

[33] Cornell Constituent Assembly, Summer Research Reports (Ithaca, N.Y.: Cornell University, 1969), I. Recommendations p. 2.

[34] Ibid., IV-B, p. 33.

[35] Ibid., V., p. 50.

[36] Ibid., V., p. 59.

[37] Quoted in Wallerstein and Starr, *The University Crisis Reader*, p. 312.

[38] While it does not yet appear that this norm is as dominant in black colleges as their white counterparts, black educators are once again playing catch-up. Howard University's Dr. Kenneth Tollett (director of the Institute for the Study of Education Policy) demonstrates a keen knowledge of market-place economics noting the "Power in this society is increasingly in the hands of the technocrats. Blacks will be frozen in a sub-class if they do not increase their numbers among the technocrats." Quoted in *Time* (September 22, 1975) p. 15.

[39] Social scientist James Coleman has recently reversed his opinion on the beneficial aspects of busing. The unpublished work of a University of Chicago social scientist purports to show the positive effects of the death penalty in reducing crime. Both of these positions have been used by Ford Administration officials to support Republican policy.

[40] Jurgen Habermas, *Toward A Rational Society* (Boston: Beacon Press, 1970 translation) p. 42.

[41] Ibid., pp. 2-3.

[42] Cornell Constituent Assembly, *Reports*, ASSP p. 4.

[43] Edna Kane quoted in *Time* (March 18, 1974) p. 81.

CHAPTER VI

Conclusion: Expanding Policy Alternatives To
Conform To Political Possibilities

The typology developed in the foregoing chapters attempts
primarily to simplify the rather complex world of racial-political
interaction in the U.S. As such, its value lies not in the possible refinements of description of past or present interracial
politics but rather in its capacity to bring out important conceptual distinctions in one of the most conceptually nebulous
areas of current American politics. Accordingly, the distinction
between the physical and the cultural, as well as that between
the nationalist and the integrationist, have been carried to their
reasonable extension. The continuities and shades of variation
between and within these extensions are nevertheless worthy of
examination. While the four categories already discussed are
both fundamental and generally sufficient for political analysis,
additional refinements or shadings are useful for accommodating
many groups whose orientations are too ambiguous or ambivalent to
fit easily into the four quadrants.

In the four quadrant typology one can easily recognize the
possibility of variations or shadings along both the vertical and
horizontal dimensions. The normative dimension, integrationism
and nationalism, need not be treated in a bipolar fashion as the
original matr_x tends to do. Similarly, the cognitive dimension
of race may be treated analytically as having physical versus
cultural extremes on a single continuum of political conceptualization. The following three figures illustrate the shadings or
rather continuities involved:

(1)

	I	N
P	PI	PN
C	CI	CN

C - cultural (cognate of race)
I - integrationism
P - physical (cognate of race)
N - nationalism

142

(2) Cognitive or   (3) Normative or
    Horizontal Continuity   Vertical Continuity

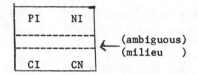

In the case of vertical continuity one comes back to the
real world inconsistency among people of unstable political
beliefs. Nationalists and integrationists have frequently
moved from one extreme to the other without ever justifying or
reconciling their various positions in terms of a central ideological focus. Martin Delany is perhaps the earliest example
of this inconsistency. Having led an effort to organize black
emigration to Africa, he chose only a few years later to run for
the United States Senate. The Delany example, however, is not
perfectly representative because it leaves aside groups whose
ideological profiles are so precarious at any moment as to place
them continually in the ambiguous vertical area.

Variations on the cognitive plane are rather more complicated,
primarily because even the extremes are only theoretically, and
not empirically, exclusive. It is virtually impossible for any
American to identify race in terms of culture without implicitly
subsuming physical characteristics as well. Still, intermingp-
ling of physical precepts in culturally oriented cognition (thinking) does not mean that the physical is primary. For example,
one could concede that any awareness of race implies a perception
of its physical aspect but all that means is that the two aspects
always occur together in the real world. Left open is the possibility that the cultural aspect of race may account for all its
social significance. The distinction may be critical for an
understanding and explication of variance in political perspectives on race.

On the other side, it seems more likely that some Americans
have maintained a uniquely physical concept of race. In fact,
many have insisted on it as the only point of view. The real
world frequency of the viewpoint, however, is easily overestimated
as a result of civil rights and related propaganda calling for
"color-blindness." Normative appeals, such as these, can distort
political language but they do not have the power to reconstitute
basic thinking without substantial intervening social transformation. For the most part, the purely physical concept can

143

only be found among those whose norms would label them as "racist," according to Pierre van den Berghe. He defines racism as follows:

> Racism is any set of beliefs that organic, genetically transmitted differences (whether real or imagined) between human groups are intrinsically associated with the presence or absence of certain socially relevant abilities or characteristics, hence that such differences are a legitimate basis of invidious distinctions between groups <u>socially defined</u> as races. . . .[1]

Evident in the above statement is the continued recourse to "social definition" even where the perspective is purely physical. Society or social relations may thus be seen as providing the environment for racial distinctions from which the racist individual draws or creates his own distorted non-social concept. Because this individual is ignoring the essentially social context of race and thereby creating a false consciousness, there appears to be a normative intent behind his redefinition. That is to say, only ideological motivation, his own or that of those he follows, can explain his digression into false consciousness.

In order to avoid politically unpleasant labels and ideological innuendo, Americans have accordingly retreated more and more toward the "conceptual center." While the center may be safe, it is in this case a very unproductive and unrewarding place to be. As we shall see, policy initiative and influence comes most often from those groups near, but not at, the extremes.

Attitudes on Blacks in Education

As has been indicated in the preceding chapters, the bulk of educational disputes in recent years are confined to the opposition of physical integrationists and cultural nationalists. In the face of opposition, however, these groups have been particularly susceptible to behavioral and attitudinal change. As indicated in Chapter 2, integrationists during the civil rights movement tended to move away from a cultural perspective on race in order to facilitate the process of legislation, which meant accommodating to views of white legislators. On the other hand, physical nationalists have tended over time to move toward a cultural perspective, largely because their revolutionary claims were on particularly shaky ground when only physical criteria could be found to legitimate them.

Of course, cognitive transformation can, and does, occur in the other directions. For example, some integrationists, whites

144

more than blacks, since the 1960s have taken the position that black children will not succeed in integrated schools unless they adopt the behavior patterns and language of whites. In other words, an important cultural distinction has been recognized, and a normative position calling for cultural integration has transformed the physical integrationists.

Some few others, starting from the same perspective, in this case blacks more than whites, have moved nearer cultural national-ism. The chapter on black studies has described such a movement in as much as students demanded some form of "academic self-determination." Of course, real questions remain as to whether the so-called demands were seriously supported and whether they were ever realistically considered.

It is in the context of these questions that the utility of ambiguous or continuous areas emerges most clearly. It is not particularly difficult to classify a group's ideology and beliefs if the group remains stable long enough for rigorous examination. In addition, it would be perfectly adequate to classify any group like the black studies advocates in one of the four quadrants, i.e. in CN in as much as its behavior and goals would conform to that of others in CN. Thus, the analyst would have to leave room for non-critical behavioral variation within each category. It might then appear that the awkward question of the usefulness of grouping black studies advocates with black separatists, like Garveyites, would remain unanswered. The answer to this question is not as complicated as it would otherwise seem if one accepts the "shaded" areas of the typology and treats them as serving a special explanatory and predictive function. Symbolically that special function is expressed by viewing the four quadrants as mutually exclusive alternatives, i.e. "A and not-A," while the shaded areas are viewed as "becoming A."

Groups in these areas, such as black studies advocates, are not only ideologically "in-between" on the typology, they are also themselves in transition. Their membership, organizational struc-ture, and ideology are in a state of development or transformation. As such, it is hypothesized that these groups have a tendency to move ideologically towards one of the four principal ideological groupings. In somewhat stronger terms, as groups develop con-sistent and active political roles they will eventually consign themselves to one of four ideological perspectives. Moreover, any sustained tendency towards another perspective eventuates in the structural reorganization or break-up of the group.

The remaining task is then to reconsider the policy making events previously discussed in the light of the latter two

145

hypotheses. In order to do so, it will be necessary to look at some groups to which only passing reference has been made--groups that have only played a marginal or incidental role in the policy-making processes discussed. As we shall see by their authoritative positions and presumed reputations, however, these groups often generally appear to be powerful or, at least, far from marginal. In most cases, potential power is mistaken for actual power. The disparity between the two reflects, among other things, the inability of a group to achieve a consistency of purpose and organization. The significance of this inability here is that political weakness is, to some extent, a consequence of the ideological malaise of many seemingly strong black interest-groups.

Perhaps the best example is the Congressional Black Caucus which seems to place itself in the ambiguous area between physical and cultural integration. Almost by definition one would expect any group of congressmen to be ideologically diversified since each congressman is supposed to represent the wishes of his own individualistic constituency. Nor would one expect a congressional caucus to behave in ways that are normally attributed to an interest-group. Yet, the basis for bringing black congressmen together is obviously the pursuit of the general interest of "the black and the poor." The Caucus's successes and failures have generally been measured more in terms of the strength of their advocacy role than in terms of their legislativ savoir-faire. Thus, it may be comparable to other black inte -groups, e.g., the NAACP, rather than to other congressional caucuses.[2]

The Caucus came into existence after, and partly as a result of, the thrust of the civil rights movements of the '60s; and there is a temptation to assume that much of the Caucus's potential program had already been taken up by others. However, one need only reflect on the Caucus's own claims--its criticisms of Washington's unresponsiveness and ineffectiveness as far as black interests may be concerned--to see that there is no lack of visible needs for the Caucus to satisfy. In fact, the Caucus's organizing of the first National Black Political Convention in Gary, Indiana, in March 1972 was an extraordinary plea for original and forceful policy initiatives.[3] Unfortunately, little originality and less force emerged from the Convention although its sessions were well attended and debate was vigorous. Still, the Convention was by no means a failure in as much as some familiar policy directions were agreed upon and a basis for organized planning was established. However, the Caucus soon disrupted this basis because of its inability to adhere to the Convention's major policy direction on education and integration.

The Black Agenda, as the Convention's principal policy statement was called, created something of a stir with its unexpected

146

pronouncement (not in the first version) on "busing." Busing in
the 1972 presidential campaign had become a major issue, and the
Convention could have had a substantial national impact, particularly if it had retained the Caucus's absolute endorsement.
Thus, the Caucus had a rare opportunity to assert unique perogatives on the major issue-offspring of the Civil Rights movement, but it declined.

The Agenda was treated in some news media as turning away
from the more traditional black insistence on integration and
"forced busing." In fact, the Agenda takes a stance of formal
indifference to busing, emphasizing instead a "quality of education" orientation and preferring black community control of schools
as priority:

> We condemn racial integration of schools
> as a bankrupt and suicidal method of desegregating
> the schools based on the false notion that black
> children are unable to learn unless they are in
> the same setting as white children. As an alter-
> native to busing black children to achieve racial
> balance, we demand quality education in the black
> community through the control of our school dis-
> tricts and an equal share of the money.[4]

The media distortion was predictable because busing, like
integration, had been reduced to an "either-or" paradigm. That
is to say, educational integration had come to be conceived of on
a national level as a physically measurable quality whose existence or absence depended solely on the ratio of blacks to whites
in the schools. The perspective implicit in the Convention is
deference to community control, actually went in a different
direction. In asserting a need for blacks to take new and independent educational initiatives, the cultural was automatically
subsumed. Perhaps as well, there was an element of nationalism
there, but the primary supposition of continued interracial
governmental authority, one step removed from the black community
intermediaries, leaves their goal still within the range of integrationism. In the main, their statement de-emphasized busing as
an issue for blacks (but not for whites), and to a lesser extent,
discredited past school integration as a basis for equal educational
opportunity. However, their concern with equality remained evident
and positive, although restrained, while the value of integrationist policy to federal government actors was still presupposed.
In sum, the only clear change represented a renewed recognition
that black-oriented modes of education should be introduced into
the public school system.

147

Partly as a consequence of the news media's sensationalistic distortion of the Agenda in labelling it "anti-busing," and partly because of its own uncertainty about the statement, the Caucus equivocated and finally rejected the "busing" statement. More profoundly, its rejection resulted from the Caucus's own ideological and identificational insecurity.

Located in the ambiguous area between quadrants PI and CI, the Caucus had been behaving before the Convention as would a physical integrationist. However, their call for an all black national political organization, with the intent of generating black policy alternatives, demonstrates their latent recognition that their socio-cultural legitimacy was not really interracial. Having thus taken the first, seemingly natural step in their development, they could not carry it through to fruition. In effect, they realized that policy could only be made at one of the extremes, PI or CI. Since they could not go that far, no policy was made.

Their immobility is apparently interwoven with the precariousness of their identity as blacks in Congress. However all-white or ethnically fragmented the Congress may have been, no other group had formally organized itself on the basis of race or ethnicity in Congress. Consequently, to be black in Congress had to mean something special. That something special was supposed to relate to issues and policy, and, thus by inference, more to the cultural than to the physical character of race. Yet, because the Caucus had not taken solid issue positions different from most liberals, e.g. Senators Kennedy or Humphrey, the criterion for membership fell to skin-color. In fact, in June, 1975 the Caucus rejected an application for membership by a white Congressman (Rep. Fortney Stark, D., Cal.) on the grounds that the CBC has "unique interests to protect and project" which does not include whites. Yet those interests have failed to manifest themselves as unique policy initiatives.[5]

Probably the solution to the Caucus' identity conflict is tied to its developing a more uniform ideological position. There is reason to believe that both of these will come in time, and that along with them will emerge a solid cultural orientation.

Serving somewhat as a stage for the display of ideological dexterity, it is understandable that no one group, including the Caucus, could dominate the Convention. As such it is a useful reference point here because it allows for the comparison of diverse groups in one setting. Notable among its non-Caucus leadership were Mayor Richard Hatcher of Gary, Indiana, and Imamu Baraka of the Congress of African People. While Hatcher seems to have played a mediating role for the public, Baraka's public profile was one of a standard bearer for various black nationalist strains.[6]

148

The nationalists, for the most part, consistently supported the busing-related statement. In particular, they more than any other group were behind the Convention's decision to de-emphasize busing and, in consequence, integration. However, their disaffection from the politics of integration never transformed itself into opposition to the policy of integration. In effect, they seemed to be saying that the policy of integration was fine as long as it was left up to others, and not themselves, to pursue it.

On the surface, such a position on a highly publicized issue smacks of indecision and ideological uncertainty. It seems, for example, to have none of the coherence of the NAACP's unrelenting emphasis on integration nor the straightforwardness of the Black Muslims' policy of racial separation. Yet, the appearance of incoherence is partly a consequence of viewing the Convention as federal government-oriented rather than as self-oriented intra-racially focused. Nationalists like Baraka, unlike the Caucus, did not seem to view the Convention as a surrogate interest-group. If abstracted from its context as an interest-group, the NAACP would also look disoriented because its largely legalistic approach to public policy requires that its own internal "policy" be one of consistent reaction, and occassional simple reflex to policy alternatives generated in the larger polity. In other words, if one limits one's policy actions to the policy initiatives of others in a specific problem area, then consistency is more easily accomplished. However, such consistency can easily lead to rigidity as it did when the national NAACP withdrew the charter of its Atlanta chapter. The Atlanta NAACP had committed the sin of agreeing to a reduction in the number of students to be bused in Atlanta in exchange for a black school superintendent and nine of 17 key executive positions in the school system.[7]

By contrast, the nationalists were attempting to do more than react to federal government policy alternatives. As such, they were trying to refocus their perogatives on "quality of education." What emerged was a sort of cultural nationalism in which integration, busing, and separatism were reduced to tactical considerations. Of course, they could not pretend to ignore the world around them, and consequently some statement on the pressing busing question had to be made. Yet, the very force of the external issue and the need to react to it corresponds to the organization's relative weakness and persistent lack, but not absence, of ideological coherence. That is to say, a single tactical position was so much more salient than any principled position on education that it obscured, and perhaps buried, the principles from which it had emerged. Pressure for a response on the issue of busing had submerged the broader issue of quality education. On the tactical issue of busing it was easy to label pro-busing forces as nationalist. Yet when the broader issue of quality education is raised, it is more difficult to attach ideological positions to the Convention participants. This does not mean, however, that such positions do not exist.

Comparatively, the physical nationalism of the Garvey movement would probably have retained its salience as a unifying core of political thought. Still, as argued earlier, physical nationalists were not able to produce a persuasive approach to separate education at the peak of the Garvey movement. It was certainly at least as unfeasible in 1972 as during Garvey's period.

Because no unifying perspective remained as important as their "indifference to busing," the Convention nationalists ended up with a position on education very much like that of Garveyites. On the one hand, they became indifferent to educational policy itself by rejecting prevailing alternatives without generating new ones of their own (possibilities are not alternatives unless some support is shown). On the other hand, there were alternatives implicit in their critique but they were devalued by the group's failure to explore them or to authorize their exploration. In the second case, the immediate possibility of black "self-determination" in education reduces to an attenuated physical nationalism--a possibility of racial separation within an otherwise formally integrated school system. The original cultural orientation of Baraka's statements is thus lost in an exclusive allusion to blacks controling education with no real consideration of how that control would differentiate black education from what might be available through busing. The only remaining criterion then for policy change is the one over which Garvey and others had floundered before.

In the long run, because there was no follow through, the Convention nationalists came to occupy that unstable hazy milieu between the two kinds of nationalism and, to a lesser degree, the one between nationalism and integrationism. It is not surprising therefore, that no strong policy influence or independent policy initiative resulted from it. For that matter, the apparent decline of subsequent conventions, in terms of attendence, may also be explained by this conceptual and normative vacillation.

Short of the Garvey comparison, the Black Muslims present a feasible policy alternative--feasible at least for thousands of blacks. Through their dual emphasis on race, genetically defined, and religion, they appear to mingle the physical and cultural concepts. But this may well be no more than appearance, the facile manipulation of images and slogans. As regards education, evidence not immediately available would be necessary to show that their cultural-religious approach to nationalism substantially penetrates their perogatives. What is evident, however, is the physical criterion of membership. What calls for special reflection in the case of the Muslims is not the salience of their criterion for race but rather the fact that their cultural character takes on a peculiarly concretized dimension.

In order to illustrate the point, one should reconsider the difference, discussed in Chapter 2, between DuBois's analytical view of culture and Harold Cruse's normative one. The first sees black culture as something to be identified and developed while the second views it as something to be created anew and disseminated among blacks. Consistent with prevailing socio-anthropological notions of culture, we have adhered to the DuBois view. What Cruse discusses under the rubric of a "cultural philosophy" is really not culture at all but rather "specific" or programmatic ideology. It resembles culture only because a global range of policy alternatives is involved. Still, it lacks the essential elements of traditional foundation and stable socialization—those things which are the framework through which learning occurs, as opposed to a collection of things which should be learned. If not ahistorical, the philosophy is, at least, anti-historical.

Along the same lines, the Muslim's cultural precepts are largely non-racial; their Islamic religion and practice are not grounded in black social history. While it is probably not devoid of black historical forebearing, as often as not one sees in the "commandments" interdictions against the things traditionally known to blacks. The desired mode of behavior is manifested and taught through the obligatory commitment to concrete symbols in eating habits, clothing, and formalized personal interaction, not to mention its reified hierarchical social structure.[8] In effect, therefore, Muslims were "made" from the raw material of blacks, physically defined, and the exclusion of whites occurred only because they are considered inadequate raw material.

Accordingly, the education of young Muslims has emphasized racial separation but the separation has not been complete. No doubt due in part to the absence of internal funds, much of their education occurs in the public school system. Yet, it is important to note that what is taught internally beyond religion is neither identified with, nor legitimated in terms of black American culture. One could go farther, and argue that Muslim education is oriented toward prevailing whites modes. This view is supported by their apparent willingness to accept educational credentials from white institutions in place of their own.[9] However, extended data, beyond the purview of the present discussion, would be necessary to substantiate this possibility as fact.

What can be judged, and what is important from the Muslim case is first that a strong physical concept of race can initially

151

serve as a basis for organization. Secondly, a cultural perspective tends eventually to emerge if a group wishes to control or affect the direction of educational institutions in an independent and creative way. Thirdly, the cultural perspective on race would, we hypothesize, tend to dominate; but it has not done so in the Muslim case essentially because they have concretized culture as religion and detached it from race. In other words, its cultural uniqueness may still be its dominant characteristic but its cultural content is not primarily founded on, nor concerned with racial identity.

In effect, the Muslims may provide "the exception that proves the rule," to the extent that ambiguity on the cultural-physical distinction is unstable may be considered a rule. Their initial development in the early 1930s was marked by the dissemination of numerous, unsubstantiated "myths of origin."[10] As with any social group, such myths can serve a valid purpose whether or not they are true. In fact, the Muslims were in competition for some time for followers with similar groups in Detroit (where they started), and the competition was characterized by the manipulation of opposing myths. The significance of this 20th century myth-making is that some cultural legitimation seems essential and a surrogate for a black tradition can serve the purpose.

As for the retention of the physical dimension, their early origins during a period of intense white racism is no doubt a primary explanation. Particularly so, because race was reintroduced into their specialized myths in the form of a religious value (the white devil). In addition, the fact that they faced competition from integrated Islamic groups suggests the utilitarian value of elevating the physical distinction. Their ambivalence on this dimension was tenable partly because their "culture" was maleable; that is, the role of race in culture was subject to management both by myth and by hierarchical authority.[11]

This kind of ambivalence in other black organized political groups, if tenable, is dysfunctional first because these others are generally engaged in conflict over "race" while the Muslims behaved as though they constituted a closed society untouched by the American mainstream. Such isolationist behavior may only be possible as long as one does not impact on the plight of the mass of blacks. In particular, as long as one does not attempt a decisive critique of the prevailing mode of education, one is more or less circumscribed. Secondly, most other groups lack the rigid hierarchical structure necessary to silence an ideologically squeamish majority. In rigidly structured groups "what is to be done" is answered for the membership. Elsewhere the way to the answer depends on "what is" and, to the extent that problems are ambiguously conceptualized, the value of any answer is compromised.

152

On the other hand, few groups have codified their ideologies in clear precise language. Lapses into ambiguity are therefore an ever-present possibility. It has been more of a probability for black than for white Americans, particularly whites in government, because the latter have maintained a fairly consistent, though unconscious approach to race as physical. Thus, a dilemma emerges in that blacks have shown a tendency to move toward the cultural approach.

The dilemma has, in large part, been fomented by the failure of legislators and administrators (mostly white) to recognize the need for an operant concept of race when they promulgate policy. This failure is best exemplified in the Ocean Hill-Brownsville controversy. Initially, the language and structure of the decentralization plan encouraged, if not presupposed, a kind of racial-cultural independence in the determination of educational goals. Blacks in this community were thus tacitly given the go-ahead to exercise their "cultural imperative." Coming to a realization of this conceptual oversight a little late, but not too late, the City, the school board, the Bundy commission, and Mayor Lindsay retracted the privilege and demanded instead that black educators behave like all other educators.

In the interim black expectations had grown. Their eventual commitment to culturally relevant education was obviously stimulated by the ambiguities of the early decentralization plan. At the same time, the retrenchment of City authorities was assured by bureaucratic and professional teacher's reliance on the most easily rationalized approach to policy implementation. As always, the concrete-physical fits best into schemes of rationalized behavior because, unlike culture, it does not require a change of behavior but simply a change of objects to which the same old behavior may be applied. In effect then, the contradictory tendencies of black and white groups along this dimension generates conflict and, in the case of Ocean Hill-Brownsville, crisis.

By contrast, conflict between nationalists and integrationists of both sorts appears to be minimal. Physical integrationists and cultural nationalists may even be disposed to accommodation in the short run because the former are likely to be indifferent to, or unaware of culturally-specific behavior. In the long run, however, the nationalist position is likely to raise the culture-consciousness of the integrationists. Such consciousness-raising was probably latent in the City's reaction to Ocean Hill-Brownsville, but real redefinition was avoided by the intervention of traditional professional groups and by the resurgence of bureaucratic rationalism.

153

The alternative outcome is that cultural nationalists will become preoccupied with the physical dimension. In fact, this pattern is implicit in the escalating demands of black studies groups for greater independence. While they seemed to be developing a cultural concept of race, at the same time the students and teachers were continually compelled to react to administrative pressures. On the one hand, faculty explications of eligibility standards for admission to black studies programs showed a disinclination for the physical. On the other hand, university administrators demanded clear-cut and hasty operational definitions of eligibility. The temptation to the physical concept thus proved irresistible.

University administrators, however, have not been uniform in their approaches. The early extension of privilege to black studies programs at Cornell brought negative reactions from some educators who believed that education must be culturally integrationist. Accordingly, Kenneth Clark's criticism of the Cornell administration is directed against the latent tendency to require cultural conformity. In the long run, it was thought that a completely integrated education was what black students needed. The solution to this university-localized conflict between cultural and physical integrationism seems to have been a complete fall back to the latter. In the interim universities had entered the nebulous plane between the two, and conflict had consequently turned into crisis.

Probably the most stable accommodation possible between the four distinctions can develop between the two kinds of nationalists. Cultural nationalists are by inclination open-minded in their critique of the other groups largely because they have not as yet been able to draw precise prescriptions for action from their rather imprecise notions of black culture. Physical nationalists, because they need to claim a revolutionary program in order to attract membership, are susceptible to any cultural claims that do not discredit their revolutionary image. In addition, the ultimate need for revolutionaries to address themselves to all aspects of social organization leads in the long run to a search for cultural legitimacy.

In the short run, however, conflict between the two is likely to develop, and historically these conflicts have often been definitive barriers to unification. The hostility between Garvey and DuBois provides an appropriate example. DuBois was clearly impressed by the Garvey movement and was supportive of it on many occassions. His supportive disposition was soon obscured by personal invectives from Garvey. Garvey, on the other hand, had tacitly recognized, through the religious-like formation of his movement, the importance of the black religious tradition; a recognition which

DuBois had given explicitly. Unfortunately for him, Garvey allowed his physical orientation to carry over into a self-conscious policy formula. Thus, revolution came to mean immediate separation, and DuBois's reservations were treated as an obstacle to revolution, as menacing as direct opposition. What is more, the very "light- ness" of DuBois's skin color was subjected to attack.

Instructive in the short term conflict between the two men is the fact that it emerged, for the most part, through personal hostilities. Without the negative personality factor it is then probable that a strong union between the two could have developed. Such a union of the apparently most adept and flexible approaches to black politics (DuBois) and the most successful in terms of organizational following (Garvey) could have had monumental conse- quences. The fact that it did not occur is significantly attribu- table to intermediaries, white and black, who deliberately aggra- vated their conflict. There is, therefore, little reason to believe that similar circumstances will not have a different outcome in the future.

What this would mean in education is perhaps most threatening for the existing school system. It would mean bringing together DuBois's call for a special approach to black education, involving both integrated and separate institutions, with Garvey's separatist preoccupation. The outcomes could only be complete separation or integration into a completely transformed social system. The latter outcome is militated by the physical nationalist's inability to countenance integration in any known form. If he is to become more tolerant then, he can not do so for education alone because his primary organizing principle would be in constant contradiction. He is therefore obliged to seek a change in the social role of education, meaning also a change in those things for which schooling is the preparation.

* * * *

It should be evident that we have, for the most part, said little about specific problems and structures in public education; for example, pedagogical alternatives have not been dealt with in any depth. In part, the need for reasonable consistency in this discussion puts specific pedogogical critique beyond the present purview. More importantly, however, any extensive concern with pedagogy runs the risk of detracting from the primary concern with race in the educational policy-making process. It is not that pedagogy and educational structures are independent of one's position on race; in fact we have argued quite the reverse. In regard to their theoretical interdependence we could perhaps have said more, but on the empirical level there is very little that needs to be dealt with separately from the policy-making process.

As previously suggested, there are no ideologically significant
variations <u>within</u> American educational structure and process.
Bureaucracies, professional groups, and specialists are over-whelm-
ingly trained to implement educational policy "without regard to
race." These same ones dominate educational structures applied to
blacks. What, therefore, reduces the need for detailed exploration
is that this same set of people and structures exercise their
politically-delegated authority over blacks in an assimilationist
manner--that is, without regard to race. The prevailing mode of
operation has been that race, however politically important, is
external to public educational administration. This suggests,
among other things, that American educators have not understood
the essentially political nature of public education. [12]

* * * * *

Finally, to briefly reconsider the anecdote in the introduction, the dilemma in the restaurant and the dilemma of blacks
in integrated schools are similar. The solution in the restaurant
was for the black to leave in rejection of his newfound integration
option. The solution in public education may well be the same.
However, it need not be so because in the restaurant the black's
despair was a response to the restauranteur's insensitivity to his
culturally defined needs and expectations. While the level of
insensitivity of most educational policy-makers is very discon-
certing, the possible cultural determinants of education for most
blacks are neither so precise nor inflexible as alternatives on
a menu may be. In addition, educators should be, in the nature
of their avowed social purpose, more open to critique and re-eval-
uation of procedures. After all, education should be the institutionalization of inspired criticism. The outcome then in education will depend significantly on the reorientation of public
education towards social criticism and evaluation--a reorientation
that would benefit both black and white students.

156

CHAPTER VI
FOOTNOTES

[1] Pierre L. van den Berghe, Race and Racism: A Comparative Perspective. (New York: John Wiley & Sons, 1967). p. 11. Underscoring is my own.

[2] See Charles Henry, "Legitimizing Race in Congressional Politics" American Politics Quarterly, April 1977.

[3] John Dean, "Black Political Assembly," Focus. II, 1. (November 1972).

[4] "Frail Black Consensus," Time Magazine, (March 27, 1972). p. 43.

[5] Ibid., (Henry).

[6] See Imamu Baraka, "Black Nationalism: 1972," The Black Scholar. 4, 1 (September 1972). pp. 23-29.

[7] See "Atlanta Blacks Trade Busing for Power" The Washington Post 3/4/73 pp. E 1-2.

[8] Malcolm X was ostensibly punished by Elijah Muhammad for having made an unauthorized impromtu remark about President Kennedy. See Rodney Carlisle, The Roots of Black Nationalism. (Port Washington, N.Y.: Kennikat Press, 1975). p. 147.

[9] Ibid. Carlisle. pp. 141-148.

[10] Ibid. Carlisle. pp. 141-148.

[11] The management of the role of race in the now World Community of Al-Islam in the West is illustrated by Eman Wallace D. Muhammad's campaign against racial images in worship. His current campaign against all racial images in worship reminds one of Father Divine's insistence on the absence of racial labels and runs directly counter to the "white devil" myth promoted by Elijah Muhammad. See "Origins of the Caucasian Christ" by Mujib Mannan Bilalian News December 16, 1977 for the last in a series of articles dealing with racial images.

[12] The number of studies which directly or indirectly support this point is far too great to list, here. They range from works of Max Weber to those of Karl Marx. For a particularly thorough analysis see: Pierre Bourdieu and Jean-Claude Passeron, La reproduction. (Paris: Les Editions de Minuit, 1970).

157